SMAHTGUY

ALSO BY ERIC ORNER

The Mostly Unfabulous Social Life of Ethan Green

The Seven Deadly Sins of Love

The Ethan Green Chronicles

Ethan Exposed

The Completely Unfabulous Social Life of Ethan Green

ILLUSTRATED BY ERIC ORNER

Love & Shame & Love by Peter Orner

Am I Alone Here? by Peter Orner

SMAHTGUY

THE LIFE AND TIMES OF BARNEY FRANK

ERIC ORNER

METROPOLITAN BOOKS

HENRY HOLT AND COMPANY   NEW YORK

Metropolitan Books
Henry Holt and Company
Publishers since 1866
120 Broadway
New York, New York 10271
www.henryholt.com

Metropolitan Books® and Ⓜ® are registered trademarks of
Macmillan Publishing Group, LLC.

Library of Congress Cataloging-in-Publication Data

Names: Orner, Eric, author.
Title: Smahtguy : the life and times of Barney Frank / Eric Orner.
Other titles: Smart guy
Description: First edition. | New York : Metropolitan Books, 2021.
Identifiers: LCCN 2021002243 (print) | LCCN 2021002244 (ebook) | ISBN
  9781250191588 (trade paperback) | ISBN 9781250191595 (ebook)
Subjects: LCSH: Frank, Barney, 1947-–Comic books, strips, etc. |
  Legislators—United States—Comic books, strips, etc. | Gay
  legislators—United States—Comic books, strips, etc. | United States.
  Congress. House—Comic books, strips, etc. |
  Politicians—Massachusetts—Comic books, strips, etc. | Comic books,
  strips, etc.
Classification: LCC E840.8.F72 O76 2021 (print) | LCC E840.8.F72 (ebook)
  | DDC 328.73/092 [B]—dc23
LC record available at https://lccn.loc.gov/2021002243
LC ebook record available at https://lccn.loc.gov/2021002244

Our books may be purchased in bulk for promotional, educational, or business use. Please
contact your local bookseller or the Macmillan Corporate and Premium Sales Department at
(800) 221-7945, extension 5442, or by e-mail at MacmillanSpecialMarkets@macmillan.com.

First Edition 2021

Designed by Kelly S. Too

Printed in China

1 3 5 7 9 10 8 6 4 2

To Blake Maher, whose love and support enabled
me to conceive, start, and finish this book.

And to my late stepdad, Mayor Daniel Pierce,
from whom I learned about politics first.

And to Dottie Reichard, who also passed away before I completed
this book. Dottie, it's not titled "Popes and Prostitutes,"
but I hope you would've liked it anyway.

AUTHOR'S NOTE

This cartoon version of Barney Frank's life is a dramatization. It combines history as I learned it and lived it working for Barney for many years, with a bit of imagination. Just as if I was creating a film or TV show, or presenting it on the stage like one of Barney's favorite musicals, *Fiorello*, there are instances where the storytelling required condensing, the use of character composites, and tinkering with the timeline to present certain events out of sequence. Some of the more personal moments employ dialogue that represents my best guess as to the words that were really used. For Barney Frank's story of record, I recommend readers seek out his wonderful autobiography, *Frank*. All that said, I did my best and tried hard not to take too many liberties.

Public business, my son, must always be done by somebody. . . .
If wise men decline it, others will not.

—John Adams

PROLOGUE
August 1989
They were hot, hungry, and pissed...
Not the way you want the national press corps to be.
WASHINGTON TIMES
SEX SOLD FROM CONGRESSMAN'S APARTMENT!

They'd been encamped in front of his apartment ever since DC's Moonie rag-masquerading-as-a-real-newspaper broke the story at 5 AM.

His car was still in the Capitol's underground lot, which meant he'd have to face the scrum, if only for the thirty-foot walk to the curb.

OMG New Sex Scandal Rocks Capitol Hill Details Tonight!

Assuming he could get a fucking cab, never a safe bet in DC.

The most nightmarish part was his own stupidity. It cut more deeply than the humiliation.

Yo, Congressman! Can we getta statement? Fuckin' hot out here!

They'd all agreed—the people he trusted most—that he'd have to answer all this shit publicly...

 Bestie
 Colleague
 Staff
 Mom
 Sibs
 Bostonians

But not today. Not here on the Hill, with the hounds yapping and baying in this insufferable August heat.

Congressman, how could you have been SO stupid??

HOW MUCH TIME DO YOU HAVE?

He'd go back to Massachusetts. He'd face them there, at home.

BOOK I

**1.
JERSEY.
1947**

Despite his Coke-bottle glasses and chunky frame, he was a popular kid in Bayonne, his hometown.

Heya, Frank, wanna play stickball?

YEAH, OK.

He was the second-eldest of four kids. His dad, Sam Frank, owned a truck stop off Route 1. His mom, Elsie, was a legal secretary.

Their working-class roots didn't mean they weren't smart, though, or politically engaged.

My Day
NEW YORK DAILY
BY ELEANOR ROOSEVELT

They revered the liberal icons of the day: FDR, Mayor La Guardia, Ben-Gurion...

What's Eleanor have to say tonight?

She's denouncing the British because they won't let that refugee ship dock in Palestine.

Good. The hell with those Brit cocksuckers. What's for dinner?

Liver & onions.

Talk about politics, sports, business, and gossip was the norm at the dinner table, on front stoops, and with neighbors clustered around their new TV.

THE KITCHEN DEBATE

Nixon's even worse than that fat commie. C'mon—let's switch to Danny Thomas.

Sam's work brought him into proximity with some of the wiseguys of the day. He briefly served time rather than testify before a grand jury about the bribery of Bayonne city officials.

But the jail stint didn't diminish Sam's patriotism, or the family's cohesiveness.

They took excursions to see tourist towns upstate...

WHAT'RE THOSE UGLY BUILDINGS, DAD?

Those are public housing towers, pal, and they're beautiful, cuz they give hardworking families a leg up!

...the monuments in DC, and college campuses in New England.

U.S. CAPITOL

WEST POINT

NEW HAVEN   CAMBRIDGE

On one of these trips, at a luncheonette in Cambridge, Mass., Sam was reading aloud an article about Adlai Stevenson. The two-time Democratic presidential nominee just happened to be sitting in the next booth. Sam didn't stop talking about it for the rest of his life.

Listen to this, kiddos. It's a quote from Governor Stevenson. Now there's a great American!

Say there, fellow, could I see that?

STEVENSON: NEW AMERICA PROGRAM

Despite the fact that most Bayonne kids stuck close to home for college—if they went at all—in 1955 his sister Ann got into Radcliffe, which was unheard of for a Jewish girl from blue-collar Jersey.

One more, honey.

Daddy, we'll miss my train.

And one day in May '57, while playing tennis with his buddies at the courts near home, his mom showed up waving a fat crimson envelope. He'd been accepted to Harvard.

Let's smoke. This'll take a while.

OH BOY!

13

He shined as an undergrad, when his fascination with government and politics blossomed in a way that wasn't uncommon at the time.

Hey, Frank, where's the fire?

Carmine DeSapio's speaking at the Law School!

That Tammany dinosaur? Can I join?

Yeah, but hurry it up. I wanna seat.

These were the years of JFK's rise to the presidency. Young people everywhere were inspired by the notion that they could help build a better America.

Barney was starting to find his own voice politically and already wasn't shy about making it heard.

The only segregation I agree with, Phillips, is inside your cortex. I favor segregating your rational ideas from your absolutely insane ones.

Increasingly, he questioned the world around him. At a classmate's parents' house in South Carolina, he made a point of drinking from a Coloreds Only fountain.

Where did you say your unusual friend is from, dear?

New Jersey.

I like him.

Soon he declared his major in government and immersed himself in every history, poli sci, philosophy, and economics elective he could squeeze in between required courses.

Social by nature, he spent time in his dorm doing his classwork and helping the other guys (no co-ed dorms back then) with theirs...

JOHN STUART MILL

Hey, Barney, what the hell does this shit mean?

HMMM

On Liberty

LEMME SEE...

...and talking endlessly about the great topics of the day...

The Harvard Crimson

SPACE RACE!

The Boston Globe

Sox lose

Rebellion in Congo

BOSTON HERALD TRAVELER

Appalling Poverty Cited in Appalachia

He cut a unique figure on campus. Friendly, sloppy, and cigar smoking.

Say there, Frank, you're wearing two different shoes.

And he so inhabited this persona as a budding political prodigy that his troubled interior life—the fact that he was secretly attracted to guys in an era when this was completely unacceptable—went undetected by others.

Hey, Barn, you dating anyone? My gal's cousin goes to Pine Manor. You up for a double date Saturday?

Sorry, better pass. Gotta cram for my ethics exam. This Hobbes and Locke stuff takes a lot outta a guy.

But that didn't mean he wasn't really scared.

If his secret came out, he'd be shamed, ostracized, an embarrassment to his family...

He'd never work in politics. That was for sure.

Time magazine had this article that kept him up at night, about an executive order singling out homos as security risks.

Some of them are very good boys. Smart, hardworking, always with a good shoeshine. But the problem, you see, is that they are subject to blackmail by the Red Menace.

President Eisenhower Reaffirms Sensible No-Perverts Policy for Federal Workforce

DATELINE WASHINGTON, D.C.

Even the Kennedys showed no interest in changing it.

Civil rights for dykes and fairies??

Sorry, gotta pass.

Hey, Frank, glad you finally agreed. Ain't she a peach?

Oh, sure. A peach...

He suppressed his true feelings. Tried dating girls. Tried passing. And he mostly succeeded. The early 1960s was an era that wasn't subtle about who was a gay man and who wasn't.

Back then, if a guy wasn't effeminate, it didn't occur to people that he could be gay...

...even if a fellow was as queeny as could be.

HAW! That Liberace's such a GAS! Huh, Elsie?

Barney was big, assertive, liked baseball...

Even one of his roommates, who confided during their sophomore year that he was gay, never suspected the same of Barney.

Barn', got something to tell you. A secret. I like guys.

OH YEAH? HUH. OK. WHATEVER.

·GULP·

Junior year, his dad died suddenly of a heart attack. Shocked and heartbroken, he left school to help Elsie settle Sam's affairs. It was critical to get a good price for the family business.

But there was a partner with whom Sam had had a falling-out, which was complicating the sale.

Barney didn't shy from taking the problem to Sam's more connected associates...

Al, a word, please?

It was taken care of.

There was enough money for Elsie and the younger kids, and for him to return to Harvard for his senior year.

TRUST Com
Pay to the order of MRS. SAM FRAN

DEED
Hudso
Ne

It was an early lesson about working the system—any system—to get a desirable outcome.

ALL ABOARD! BOSTON!

Barney, go. We'll be fine.

At the grad school of government he became a popular resident tutor and a student activist—a sort of political polymath...

...as concerned with social justice at home as he was with human rights and development abroad.

He gravitated toward other idealistic young people.

HEYA, GANG!

Oh, good! Barney, explain to this lunkhead the essentiality of Lenny Bruce.

An anonymous foundation paid the airfare for student activists to attend gatherings in far-flung places like Scandinavia...

...where the World Festival of Youth and Students was held in 1962.

Years later it turned out the CIA had footed the bill—part of a sneaky scheme to co-opt student activists.

Somewhere in Langley

We need more flyers for Columbia, Harvard, and Brown.

Yes, Colonel.

Gloria Steinem was another student at the conference, though they weren't close.

Mind if I smoke?

Not if you share.

Only have cigars.

Gotta problem with girls smoking cigars?

Nope.

OK then.

2. EXPANDING HORIZONS

BRUTAL MANDATE by ALLARD K. LOWENSTEIN

He was wowed when a fiery young writer came to campus to talk about Afrikaner rule in South Africa...

...and volunteered to drive the author around Cambridge for the rest of the weekend.

I'm embarrassed to admit I've never thought much about injustice in South Africa.

You and 99% of our fellow Americans. At least you're interested now.

They just clicked, sharing outrage at reactionary politics at home and around the globe...

Hell no. The dean's.

Nice wheels. Yours?

...and a commitment to...

...advancing liberal values...

...and something more maybe, a sort of deferred loneliness—putting their passion into politics and activism.

GOTTA USE TH' JOHN

Cuba Congress LBJ The British Labour Party

They stayed in touch, writing, swapping ideas, talking on the phone.

Allard, it's really late.

Too late to fight unconstitutional racism? Should I call back after, what, 4:30 AM?

Nevertheless, I need a deputy, and know there's nothing you believe in more than the right to vote. So get your Greyhound ticket, you're coming!

Phone

I'm going to Mississippi with a bunch of students. Want you to join us.

The only thing this Jerseyite would rather not do than go to Mississippi is go to Mississippi in the summer.

Mississippi in 1964 was a scary and dangerous place for student activists. Three young freedom fighters were murdered. Their bodies were discovered by the FBI, buried in a swamp.

DEAD BLACK & JEWISH STUDENTS

HUMIDITY

ENTERING MISSISSIPPI

DEAD POSSUM

DEAD FROG

Allard got in a fight with other activists over tactics and wound up not going.

Barney went anyway, gamely going door-to-door registering voters.

So that's why it's critical to register with the **Mississippi Freedom Party**.

Say what now?

With his thick Jersey accent, though, and his spitfire way of talking, he had some trouble making himself understood.

Sorry, young feller, but the missus and I are not quite catchin' you.

Not quite catchin' you a'tall.

The coordinating committee decided canvassing might not be what he was best cut out for.

So, um, Brother Barney. Thanks for your efforts—you're a great man. But we may have a different job for you.

It was hard not to notice all the good-looking activist guys.

Instead, they sent him to the state capitol in Jackson, to help draft a petition establishing the new Mississippi Freedom Party.

The new party would challenge the Mississippi Democratic Party's selection of an all-white delegation to the 1964 Democratic National Convention in Atlantic City and offer instead a slate of pro-civil rights delegates.

At the end of the summer, Barney went up to DC to show his work to Joe Rauh, the famous civil rights attorney coordinating the freedom fighters' legal efforts.

Could we use this?

Doubtful. But it's a better idea than I've had all day.

Not a lawyer, are you, son?

Uh-uh, sir. Why?

Because by the time you and I finish indicting these crackers...

...their friends in DC will surely have found some way to disbar you.

Got any other skeletons rattling around in your closet?

Ha ha, no, sir, don't think so.

When the convention finally assembled in August, however, it rejected Rauh's petition.

Weyauh vote no NIGRA delegates from Mississippi.

So was their vote count, son, and that's the coin of the realm.

But our arguments were bullet-proof.

At the White House, a furious President Lyndon Baines Johnson barked at his lieutenants to find a compromise.

Ah want harmony at mah convention!

Offer the coloreds two delegate slots.

But the Mississippi Freedom delegates rejected LBJ's deal.

We didn't come all this way—

Part of him thought: two delegates are better than zero delgates.

But he was moved (along with about half the country watching on TV) when one lady said:

—for no two seats.

Fannie Lou Hamer

3.
CRIMSON
COCOON

Freedom Summer ended. LBJ was elected in a landslide, then rammed the Voting Rights Act and Medicare and Medicaid through Congress. As exciting as it had been to be at the white-hot center of national debate, it was a relief to be back on campus...

A. J. Liebling

SCULL

...where more variation from the social norm was tolerated than in the wider world.

But politics aside, why don't you have a sweetheart?!

Sure, he'd occasionally date women, often those with whom he shared a passion for social issues, if not romance or sex.

Darling, let's join the Peace Corps together.

It was a relief when these relationships ended.

POP

Other than
the occasional trip to
the newsstand in Harvard Square to check
out the wrestling magazines, he mostly
tried to bury the thoughts he had
about sexual desire and men.

It was enough, he told himself, to play tennis or squash with guys he would have liked to like.

Gotta quit, Barn'. Penny 'n' me are gonna catch the new Hitchcock. Wanna join?

Nah, thanks though.

It also helped to throw himself back into grad student life.

And to begin his thesis.

For which he was still without a topic.

But political life kept interfering.

For one thing, Allard was always cooking up something.

A bus to where? I dunno, Al, I gotta lotta work to do.

Talking Barney into tagging along at this activist conference or that...

...where their friendship and admiration for each other continued to grow.

You gonna speak?

Should I?

Hell yeah!

POWER TO THE PEOPLE, MAN!

Encampment for Citizenship summit, Riverdale, NY, 1965

In 1966, during his last year of grad school, he was appointed assistant director of Harvard's Institute of Politics.

The new job involved a lot of thankless tasks...

But it also exposed him to some of the leading figures of the day.

Like Defense Secretary McNamara, who came to explain why it was in our national interest to bomb Vietnamese villages.

And he became more adept at the nuts and bolts of managing public events. The scheduling, the logistics, and the messaging. Some of the high-profile types who came to campus asked him to take on special projects...

Hey, Barney, good job with the McNamara event. He's a pig, but still, nice job.

Actually, Frank, it was really well organized.

Yes. Nice going.

You're Frank, right? The name's Dukakis. Wonder if you'd like to help our progressive study group up at the State House.

All of which pulled him away from starting his thesis, and building an academic career to earn himself a living.

-1-

4.
Kevin
Versus
Louise

He started to get invites where he rubbed elbows with local media celebs, activists and pols.

Chris Lydon, meet Barney Frank. You should get on famously. You both eat, sleep, and breathe *Politics!*

The talk was about Vietnam and civil rights and poverty and... Nantucket.

Same place I winter. Roxbury.

Oh, right on.

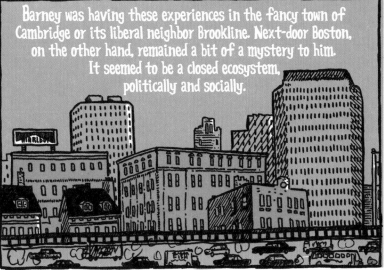

Barney was having these experiences in the fancy town of Cambridge or its liberal neighbor Brookline. Next-door Boston, on the other hand, remained a bit of a mystery to him. It seemed to be a closed ecosystem, politically and socially.

Oh sure, it was mostly as diverse as any other big city—with Italians and Jews, Blacks and French Canadians, folks of Chinese ancestry, others from Portugal...

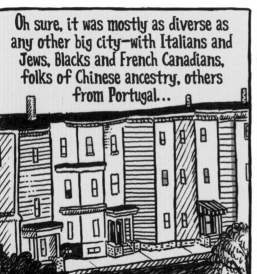

...as well as its annual full-scale invasion of students from everywhere under the sun.

It had its world-class museums, like the Isabella Stewart Gardner...

It had Yaz hitting homer after homer at Fenway...

...a busy international airport...

...and the Pops.

...Bill Russell amazing his fans at Boston Garden...

...and a famously creaky mass transit system.

And hundreds of brilliant kids graduating each year from places like MIT and going on to tech pioneers like Wang Labs, Digital Equipment, and Lotus.

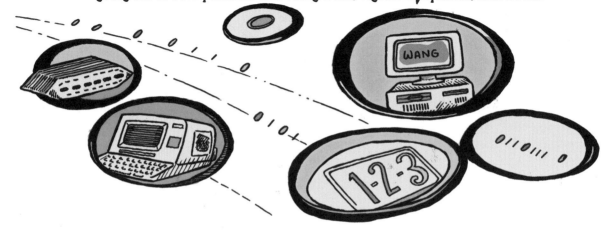

But despite all these attributes of a world-class city, in Boston in the mid-1960s, if you weren't Irish Catholic...

...if you or your dad or grandpa hadn't been a sworn friend or blood enemy of the late mayor James Michael Curley...

(This book's not about him, but it's worth knowing how important he was in the years before Barney got to town.)

...hadn't taken part in the decades-long Hibernian carnival that was Curley's dominance over Boston...

...well, friend, then you were *nobody*. And as the bosses of the era used to say: *We don't want nobody nobody sent.*

Despite the ossified political landscape, the physical one was changing fast. Old neighborhoods were bulldozed in the name of progress and urban renewal.

Near the waterfront, block after block of tenements, dives, and mom 'n' pops (and more dives) had been leveled to make way for the new Government Center...

Now where will we getta drink?

Or see a girlie show???

Or place owa bets?

Curse you, urban renewal!

BUILDING A BETTAH BOSTON

...from which a giant, and giantly ugly, concrete pile that was Boston's new city hall rose.

VIVA BRUTALISM!

Isn't it splendid!

BUILDING A BETTAH BOSTON

30

In 1967 a new mayor was to be elected. Business backed a guy who'd championed the Government Center project, and promised more like it.

Vote for me.

Yeah. Vote for him.

But like civic-improvement types since time immemorial, this candidate seemed to like humanity better than actual humans. The voters, in their wisdom, felt the same way about him.

Not feelin' it.

Us neithah.

Instead, defying the polls, the experts' prognostications, the condemnation of the *Boston Globe*, and the hopes of the town's liberal elites, the September "preliminary" election resulted in a reactionary dam breach known as *Louise Day Hicks*...

...a daughter of South Boston, the tough white working-class neighborhood near the harbor. Louise married young, raised a family, and, remarkably for a Southie matron of the 1950s, went to law school. Soon, she got elected to the school board...

Roxbury schools need textbooks!

And PLUMBING!

ORDER!

...where she quickly became chairwoman, and an unyielding voice of resistance to a changing city—especially Black citizens' demands for fair treatment.

There is no segregation in Boston schools.

White women can no longer walk the streets of Boston in safety.

YOU KNOW WHERE I STAND!

"The Lady" cut a startling figure. A large woman with a baby-doll face and a bouffant hairdo, she dog-whistled—or blowtorched—her message. And it resonated, not just in Southie, but across the city.

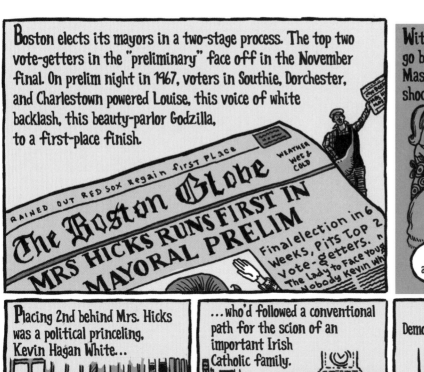

Boston elects its mayors in a two-stage process. The top two vote-getters in the "preliminary" face off in the November final. On prelim night in 1967, voters in Southie, Dorchester, and Charlestown powered Louise, this voice of white backlash, this beauty-parlor Godzilla, to a first-place finish.

RAINED OUT RED SOX Regain First Place

The Boston Globe

WEATHER WET & COLD

MRS HICKS RUNS FIRST IN MAYORAL PRELIM

Final election in 6 weeks, Pits Top 2 vote-getters. The Lady to Face Young Nobody Kevin wh...

With only six weeks to go before the final vote, Massachusetts liberals were shocked.

More wine?

Better open another bottle.

Placing 2nd behind Mrs. Hicks was a political princeling, Kevin Hagan White...

...who'd followed a conventional path for the scion of an important Irish Catholic family.

The son and grandson of Democratic grandees and a graduate of Williams College, Kevin had parlayed...

The kid could blow this thing if he don't get offah his ass.

Gramps says you'll lose to Louise if you don't get off your ass.

...good looks and the family name into statewide office almost before the ink had dried on his law diploma. He was smart, if not particularly suave, like a guy in an Old Spice ad.

Thanks, Pop. Heard him the first time. Just recharging.

And he was charming. When he wanted to be. Which wasn't always.

Kathy?
Hey, Kath?

Kevin White didn't love the political hustings like his old man. He didn't mind the half-assed way his brother was "managing" the campaign—giving the candidate several nights off a week to spend with his lovely wife...

Are they gone?

For the time being.

...rather than being out pressing the flesh at some wake or fish fry.

Here's some flesh I like pressing.

Mmm. You should listen, y'know. Do more events.

Oh God, not you too.

Which is why, if elected, I will give 30% raises to owa police officahs and fiya fighttas.

And that was a problem, because with only six weeks until the election, Louise was picking up steam.

Which greatly concerned "the Vault," a secretive club of the city's richest bankers and lawyers, whose members didn't like what The Lady's populism might mean for their business climate. So they joined forces with Boston's liberals to back Kevin and inject some professionalism into his campaign.

What we need, gentlemen, is a political operative for the unenviable privilege of bringing order to the chaos of an attractive, if lazy, candidate's **schedule messaging.**

Thanks for coming.

And, as is the case with every politician this group has ever dealt with, **financing.**

34

Your Honor!

Might be a little premature for that, Chris.

Yeah, about that: word around town is you could maybe use a little help keeping the trains running on time. Look, I don't want to tell you how to run your campaign, but I know a kid who might be of use.

Christopher Lydon, local media celebrity

BRIE & CHABLE of Charles St.

ANTIQUES

MASS 803·234

Across the river at that very same moment.

The next day, in the city

A college kid? I dunno, this thing's gettin' tighter by the day.

Yeah, what we DON'T need is some Ivy douchebag flakin' out ovah a weekend because he'd rathah chase tail than organize the shite we need organized.

Relax, will yas both. I'm gettin this direct from my guy at the bank. Says some shit at Harvard, talking head TV guy or somethin', made the recommendation. Supposed to be a real whiz kid. **Smaht.** Lotta energy. But fat. No social life at all. I'm hearin' this kid'll live an' breathe the work that you don't wanta do yourself.

35

Thesis still hovering around page one

So, he got a call summoning him across the river, to meet the candidate on Beacon Hill.

Really? Well, OK. Gimme the address.

His motivation for agreeing was entirely negative.

He was appalled by Louise Day Hicks's racist demagoguery.

huh...

So fearful of sharing her city with anyone who was different.

He also felt fearful.

FOOMP

Because not a day had gone by since he was, what? Fifteen? When he wasn't acutely aware of how *different* HE was.

Anyway, he felt obligated to make sure she was defeated.

True to the rap he was getting around town, the candidate ran way late.

C'mon in then. Don't touch nothin'!

Mt. Vernon St., Boston

After ten minutes alone in the den of Kevin White's town house, Barney started thumbing through a pretty terrific library.

Then the old ward boss sharpened his cue and offered some advice: "First Rule of Politics, kid. Don't talk too much. If you can nod it, don't say it. An' if you can wink it, don't nod it."

Barney was so engrossed, he didn't notice an hour later when the man finally appeared.

Hey, pal, you wanta do this interview or what?

OH HEY! Sure! Hope it's OK I took a look at your books.

Whadd'ya got? *Ward Eight*? About how Martin Lomasney ran the West End from his pool hall? Love that one. The old bastard sure had his hands full—back when the whole town was covered with IRISH NEED NOT APPLY signs...

Did'ja ever meet him?

But my father-in-law helped send him off at a torchlight parade. Or so he says. Anyway, all that old-timey, ward-heeler shit? Those ways are finished.

Lomasney?! Mother of God, kid, how old do you think I am? I was like, what? Five when the Mahatma—that's what everyone called him—finally croaked.

I want to open the goddamn city up! I want everybody in the motherfucking tent! I want the Blacks! I want the Puerto Ricans! I want the Portuguese and the Chinese and the Cape Verdeans and the friggin' Wampanoags. Hell, I want the fairies and the dykes.

He'd gone to the meeting with low expectations—assuming Kevin White was just another young pol on the make. But he was impressed.

KOFF

Kevin's instincts on racial issues, on economic fairness, on the neighborhoods—not just downtown—all seemed genuine. And wow, he was so charismatic. After talking for over an hour (jeez, who ran the man's schedule?), Barney held out his hand.

Well, OK then, I'm willing to help out.

Ha! I thought you were the interviewee, not the other way around.

The candidate liked this smart, presumptuous kid and hired him.

Hey, kiddo, whattabout my book?

Oh!

That's OK. Keep it.

Really?

See ya tomorrow.

I'll be in around 10 AM-ish. But you be there by 8.

The campaign was ripe for wresting from Kevin's brother, whom local wags called Raoul after Fidel Castro's gloomy sibling...

Where's Kevin?

At some event in Jamaica Plain.

An' what th' hell're you doing?

Minding the store, Pops.

Listen, Raoul, we need a little help for the last leg.

SCHPRITTT

Within a few days, Barney was bringing a whiz kid's energy and drive to the campaign's final stretch.

Suddenly, the house parties were well attended...

And modern!

Isn't he HANDSOME!

Thanks for staying late, ladies!

There's pizza.

The donations were properly banked and the campaign's checkbook balanced nightly...

What's this?

Your position on low-rise housing at Methunion Manor.

Didn't know I had a position.

I took the liberty.

Good lad.

Elect Kevin WHITE Mayor of Boston

CITGO

The key intersections had volunteers holding signs during the AM and PM rush...

And the candidate's speeches were drafted in time for him to review them before learning what he had to say about a sensitive topic in real time in front of an audience.

All this new efficiency gave Kevin room to finally get into a campaign groove.

He began to exploit Louise's mistakes—like the fact that no way did the city's coffers have the cash for the raises she'd promised cops and firefighters.

Aw, c'mon. You know that's BS, madam.

I know no such thing!

She'd traveled down to DC to secure federal money to back up her commitment. But no one down there would meet with her.

Really?

Yup.

Huh...

Since he was basically nobody—not Irish, not Catholic, not a member of some powerful Southie or Dorchester or West Roxbury clan nursing an ancient grudge—Barney's ascendancy as an important campaign advisor didn't come at the expense of anyone who mattered. He was the political equivalent of an excellent maid dispatched to bring order to a household at odds over who'd clean the basement. As long as he did the job, the different factions in Kevin's orbit were happy to let him keep at it.

KEVIN for MAYOR!

It's a reporter from *Time*. Says he wants to talk to the campaign manager.

Let's let the whiz kid take it, Raoul.

Racism had a lousy night.

And then, as suddenly as his involvement with the campaign had begun—it was over. Kevin White had eked out a narrow victory on election night.

It had been exhilarating and exhausting.

And also, somehow, safe. When a guy's working 24/7 doing something rewarding, he's not lonely.

Smoke?

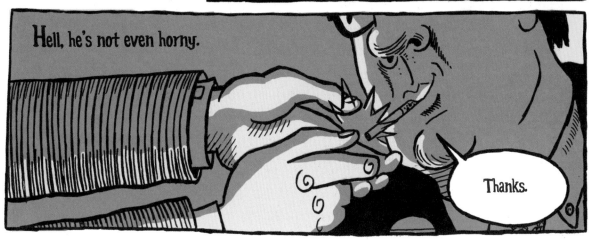

Hell, he's not even horny.

Thanks.

But it was over now and he was trying to convince himself that he was glad to get back to that ream of blank paper next to his Smith Corona with only a year left to turn in his PhD thesis.

Kevin, however, was having none of that.

Christ, whatrya doin' out here? Boss wants you.

NOW.

City Hall = mucho pussy.

GLUG

WHAT?!
Listen, chief, you're not going anywhere if I can help it, except a dingy f'ing office in that gawdawful new City Hall to help me run this motherfuckin' town.

Gee, I'm flattered, Kevin. But I can't do it.

Sure you can, kiddo. Just say:

"Yes, Mr. Mayor."

One of you boneheads help Kathy with the TV.

I wanna hear the Dragon Lady's concession.

Almost have it, Daddy.

Compliments of BOSTON STAEDTLER HILTON

Campaigns make it look so easy. "Elect me and I'll immediately do X, Y, and Z." Then the winner discovers the thousand and one reasons why promises made on the campaign trail aren't easily achievable...

Even so, the new mayor wanted change everywhere. Police brutality, redlining in housing, school segregation, blighted neighborhoods, disenfranchised Bostonians with no say in how the city was run...

And if Kevin's family were practitioners of old-style politics...

...all the more reason for Kevin to want an outsider hiring the experts he needed to realize his vision.

**5.
Whiz Kid
at City Hall**

So Barney took the job. Mornings he'd race to the subway, passing insurance men, advertising men, PR women, and secretaries on their way to work; construction guys getting coffee and rolls; night nurses from Mass General dead on their feet...

Where's the fire, young man?

I'll know when I get to work, Sister!

As he emerged from the station, City Hall would fill his field of vision as if a huge cement spaceship had set down in old Scollay Square.

Barney was in charge of scheduling, communications, administrative departments, and lobbying councillors to approve the mayor's agenda. He was the point man on big projects like the expansion of Logan Airport and an interstate highway extension through Boston. He was the mayor's eyes and ears at political events, and spent hours poring over résumés from urban affairs experts who'd been inspired by Kevin's campaign.

Morning, Barney.

Mmmphft.

As promised, his office was a hellhole. Although it rated highly, being next to the mayor's suite.

Morning, Polly.

Morning, Mr. Segel.

Is he in?

Does he look in?

Jim Segel, City Hall Assistant

His desk was a Matterhorn of papers, binders, coffee cups, and Hostess wrappers, though he insisted he knew where everything was and barred the cleaning crew from tidying up.

Looks good, Segel.

A member of the secretarial pool was assigned to wrangle his phones, which rang incessantly, all day long. Everyone wanted Barney because everyone knew he had the mayor's ear.

Councillor Langone on line three.

Vendors wanting city contracts.

Heck, we'd love to have the mayor c'mon over to see our process.

Union officials shouting complicated grievances.

Federal bureaucrats alleging compliance violations.

Mr. Frank, are you familiar with Section 32A (b) (vii)?

Political supporters pissed something hadn't been done, said, or taken care of.

His mom called a lot also.

When I think of the mothers losing their sons in some jungle FOR WHAT?

Newsweek

He had a special way with people who weren't bigwigs—Joe Nobodies who often turned out to have legitimate beefs with city government. He identified with them. He was a nobody himself. Or worse than a nobody, given his sexual desires. But nobody knew about that. (And it was gonna stay that way.)

What's your son's name? And the police brought him to which station?

In school he'd studied government and politics as positive forces in the lives of citizens—people banding together to tackle problems too big to be handled by one person (or family, or corporation, or state); stuff like mass transit, education, financial help for laid-off workers. His new job let him put this belief into practice. And he loved it.

Agree. No one should be treated that way. We'll look into it and get back to you by the end of the week.

Yeah, promise.

G'nite. See you in the morning.

After 6 PM, most of the Hall cleared out. He'd sit in his bunker of an office and look out through little slit windows at the town's two famous old derelicts, Faneuil Hall and Quincy Market.

Kevin had talked to urban design types about turning the market into a tourist attraction. Barney didn't think out-of-towners were dying to wander around Boston's old fish-monger stalls. But aesthetics weren't exactly his area, so he kept his mouth uncharacteristically shut.

He liked turning up the police radio in the mayor's outer office; traffic in the Callahan Tunnel, a fire on Dorchester Ave., flower children overdosing on the Common.

It was amazing what you could learn about a place from the scanner. Boston hadn't been his home, but that seemed to be changing.

6.
MLK

On a Thursday evening, four months into the job, he and a few staffers were holed up in a conference room.

So let's see the budget summary for our summer jobs proposal.

KNOCK KNOCK

One of the secretaries burst in...

The police scanner is saying that that Dr. King has been shot!

Somebody turn on a TV! Fuck—where's the mayor??!

OH NO OH NO OH NO

Mayor kicked off early, said he was takin' the missus to the picture show.

SHIT! Go get him!

Been lookin' forward to this flick, maybe we should sit tight, an—

GODDAMN IT, SOMEBODY FIND THE MAYOR!

I'll take the stairs.

It was pandemonium. The TV was reporting Dr. King's murder and spontaneous rioting across the country. Phones in City Hall were ringing off the hook. Kevin was fished out of a movie house and rushed off to police headquarters...

Horror in Memphis this evening.

CBS

...while Barney worked on a mayoral statement.

The assasination of Martin Luther King is a tragedy that diminishes us all.

A few hours later, a tour bus carrying white passengers was blocked by Black demonstrators on Blue Hill Avenue. Barney, on the phone with the mayor and the police commissioner, argued against an armed response...

Instead, they reached out to local clergy, who, to everyone's massive relief, resolved the standoff peacefully. Even so, the city was a tinderbox threatening to ignite all night and into the next day.

After a sleepless night at City Hall, morning brought a new complication.

Barney, you better take this.

A DJ passed on a rumor that the James Brown concert scheduled for that night would be canceled by Boston Garden.

I need to speak with the mayor.

At first, no one got the significance.

James Black? Is he a rock 'n' roll star?

Brown. James BROWN, Mayor.

Maybe it's not a bad idea. To cancel. Outta respect...

I'm afraid y'alls missing th' point, Mr. Mayah.

Garden Management's right. They don't need 5,000 hoodlums trashing the place.

Concert's tonight. Too late to get the word out. You're gonna have thousands of youths show up at the Garden. They're gonna be pissed. And with Dr. King—they're already pissed. Situation's combustible!

What the fuck do we do now? Ideas, people?

Mayor, we gotta plead with this singer to go on as planned...

Yes, this is Mayor White of Boston—hoping to speak with Mr. Black's management team...

Rioting in Detroit, Newark, and Washington, DC!

BROWN! *MR. BROWN'S* TEAM!

They enlisted public TV to televise the concert...

It'll help keep the kids offa the streets tonight.

WGBH

Tell the mayor that for the good of the community, we'll do it.

But the record label countered that televising would depress earnings at the gate, which meant James Brown would charge the city more.

HOW MUCH MORE?

Ten grand,* brother.

BONK

*About $76,000 in today's dinero.

Only when Brown had been met by the mayoral limo and rushed to the Garden...

...with an arena full of young people whistling and calling for him to take the stage, did they finally strike a deal...

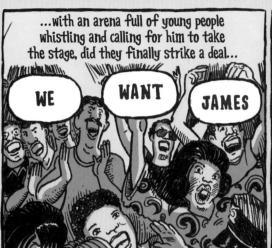

WE WANT JAMES

...backstage, with roadies shouting at them not to touch amps or step on cords. The mayor wound up guaranteeing James Brown an extra ten grand.

The deal having been brokered, the mayor was invited onstage...

...to introduce, and kiss the ass of...

...the Godfather of Soul for gracing the city with his presence during the national tragedy.

Brown took the stage and admitted to the crowd that he had never heard of Kevin an hour before, but had discovered the young mayor to be a:

Pretty Swingin' Cat! YEAH! Now Let's pray For Martin.

To everyone's bottomless relief—and unlike other northern cities in the aftermath of Dr. King's murder—little violence broke out in Boston that night, or in the nights that followed.

The mayor's staff spent the next few months plugging the hole that the concert had blown in the budget...

Do you folks **really** need me here?

Yes, Mayor.

To make decisions on what to cut.

Ultimately, they turned to The Vault.

Let me put it this way, gentlemen. Unlike your brother bankers elsewhere, you still have a city to lord it over.

Which is why I need a million-dollar donation to be set aside for programs to ease racial tensions.

DEAL.

We'll give you $100,000 for summer jobs.

F'ing liberals.

Months passed, then a whole year. The mayor threw more and more at Barney.

Mayor needs you to review this before his 2 o'clock.

His political acumen, problem-solving skills, and outsider status (without a stake in all the Irishy clan infighting) meant he quickly became the mayor's most relied-upon aide.

You fellahs wanta sit in on the Little City Halls planning meeting?

FUCK YOU, GRAMPS.

We'll pass, whiz kid.

Something the papers began to notice.

THE BOSTON PHOENIX

MEET The MAYOR'S RIGHT HAND

TALKS TOO FAST

Smart

From JERSEY OF ALL PLACES

DOES HIS HOME-WORK

Acerbic

Husky

And since Kevin was more of a big-picture guy, the day-to-day management of the city was increasingly left to Barney and a few others.

Hi, folks. Mayor sends his regrets. Let's get started.

7.
Daily
Grind

He almost never took time off, except for maybe a few hours some mornings following all-nighters at the Hall.

Hey, big shot.

When's your boss gonna do sumfin about these gawdamn buses?

Corner Spa

FOOD CENTER

PEPSI

WHITE BREAD 3 in 1.00

What's wrong with 'em?

HUFF

They nevah fuckin' come, for stahters.

Hey, Angie, where's the Cup O' Noodles?
Aisle two on the bottom, Barn, but you shouldn't eat it. Loaded with sodium.
Yeah, yeah.
You gotta do something about the Blacks, Bahney. They're gettin' too big fowa their gawdamn britches.
Cut the racist crap, Gus. Or I'll find another crap store to shop in.
POP-Tart
DOLLAR CINEMA
Ma, I can't talk. Any minute the mayor's gonna—
Oh, that mayor of yours can wait five minutes for you to talk to your own mother!
And when he's done waiting you can tell him...
...to do something about inner-city schools! I've been reading *Newsweek*. Barney, do you know the dropout rate for Black teenagers in this country?
ELLERY QUEEN
LAWS OF THE COMMONWEALTH

Sigh. Thirty percent.
Well, if you already know, why aren't you doing more about it?!
CHIME
Hold on, I've got the Fuller Brush guy at the door.
TIMES CROSSWORD BOOK
OUR BODIES, OURSELVES
WRIGLEY'S DOUBLEMINT
LEFTY HOUSE ORGAN

I'm back. Are you eating right?
Sure, Ma.
I'll bet. Sounds like you have a mouthful of Pop-Tart.
HONK HONK
HEY BAHNEY.
BEAT A FUCKIN' EGG! MAYOR'S IN THE CAH WAITING ON YOUR ASS.
ARMY NAVY
BARNEY, DON'T FORGET TO TELL THE MAYOR ABOUT THE SCHOOLS!
Gotta go, Mom.
Motheragawd, what's takin' him so long?
Dunno, Mayor. Maybe he's on the phone with that pinko battle-ax mom of his back in Jersey.
Well, toot the fuckin' horn again, will ya?
HONK HONK!

Most days he'd work late,

finally calling it quits around 7 PM.

DAMN THING ATE MY QUARTER AGAIN!

Doing you a favor. Chocolate bar ain't no proper dinner, Bahney.

Then he'd trudge home for a TV dinner or leftover Entenmann's cake from breakfast, or sometimes just a Snickers from the Hall's larcenous vending machine.

He liked the summer nights when people left work and headed down to the river...

...or just sat on their stoops like they did in Bayonne, taking in whatever breeze they could...

sigh. Nice view.

Hey, smahtguy, my granddaughter's school's gotta 'bouta hunert broken windows. The freakin' starlings make nests in the kids' hair.

He wasn't a guy to waste time, but stopping to chat made him feel less lonely. And since his neighbors knew he worked for the mayor, he got an earful.

I'll call the school department in the morning.

Got another cigar?

Call first thing.

His route home took him down the last block of Arlington—behind the Public Garden and its swan boats. (Why anyone would want to paddle around in those things was beyond him.) He'd heard that this stretch was known for male hustlers. Or maybe as a cruise area. Or both. He wasn't sure.

But he'd never seen anything there other than a normal block of brownstones.

On one of these summer nights, he was on this block headed home when he noticed a streetlight was out...

...and he was making a mental note to call the BTD* the next day... ...when someone tapped him on the shoulder.

Hey, man.

Sorry, didn't mean to startle you. Gotta light?

Oh. Uh—sure...

* Boston Transportation Department

He fumbled around for a lighter.

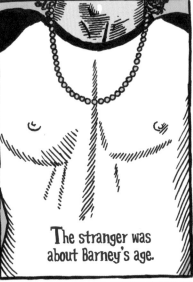

The stranger was about Barney's age.

In better shape, though.

He was holding a tennis racket.

Which he caught Barney glancing at.

Thanks for the light, man. **You play?**

Uh, haven't in a while. Used to play in high school...

Oh yeah? When was that? Couple of years ago?

Jeez, is this guy *flirting* with me?

Not quite, haha.

You know those courts on the other side of the Common?

Yeah, sure.

Wanna meet tomorrow night around 7? Hit a few balls?

Um, sure. Yes.

I'm Carl.

Barney.

OK, Barney. Looking forward to it, man.

His heart was practically leaping out of his chest as he walked the rest of the way back to his apartment. He was pretty sure that for the first time in his life, he had a REAL DATE.

Panel 1:

The next day was interminable...

Coming?

Where?

Interagency meeting you called.

Swell.

SKRATCH.

Panel 2:

...meetings about press strategy...

The *Herald* and *Phoenix* do nothing but snipe at our Little City Halls plan. It's very demoralizing.

Panel 3:

...about parks (with an agenda bullet—here was an irony—about finding money to resurface tennis courts)...

AGENDA

RESURFACE TENNIS COURTS

Panel 4:

...about crumbling schools in Dorchester and Roxbury.

HEY KEVIN DEIUX

WE DEMAND ACTION

Now

CRACKIN

Leaky classrooms

Panel 5:

At 6:03 PM he told Segel:

Heading out.

Huh?

Panel 6:

Since when does he play tennis...

Sure, Barn. Uh, have fun...

Panel 7:

Who said anything about fun?

Uh. Nobody.

Right. OK. See you in the AM.

Panel 8:

Sitting on the crappy metal bleachers beside the courts, he watched Carl approach. The guy had a great build. Strong, but graceful. Like a quarterback.

Glad you showed! Had my doubts. HAHA. Ready ta play?

He wore a stars-and-stripes sleeveless shirt that was both subversive and a bit fruity. And he had arms that were hard not to stare at.

They played a couple of pretty competitive sets. Carl won the first...

...but Barney slashed and huffed his way in the second, closer battle...

...after which they called it quits. It was closing in on 9 PM, but still in the mid-80s on the Common.

That was great!

It was! Wanta sit on the bleachers for a while?

schpritt

Would love to, man, but I gotta date tonight. So, gotta fly. But you free same time on Thursday?

Hopes dashed, and then almost as quickly redeemed, he agreed.

Later, Barney.

Later, Carl.

Hot enough for ya, Barney?

Yup.

On Thursday, Boston was still in the middle of a heat wave. Wherever he went, it was like standing behind a bus.

Nervous before this second tennis date, he stopped at the Store 24 on Boylston Street and devoured some snack cakes...

They volleyed for a while, then played a set, which Carl won, but only after pretty contested games (Barney always being a more athletic competitor than his husky frame might suggest).

After, they found a spot to sprawl out on Boston Common—which on this summer night was crowded: flower children, winos, students, kids leafletting, cops on horseback,

and weirdly for nighttime, *squirrels*. Maybe they were disoriented by the heat, but whatever their reasons, there were a lot of squirrels...

Carl had a pack of peanuts. He scattered a few in front of him...

One of the squirrels scooped them up and ran away.

I wonder where he's dashing off to.

In this neighborhood? Probably another SDS meeting.

Huh?

Squirrels for a Democratic Society.

HAW! You're fuckin' funny, man!

THRILLED, THEN SCARED →

I LOVE funny guys!

HEY, uh, not so *public*. There's cops over there.

So what?

Maybe we could go somewhere? My place is just a few... but, wait, my landlady.

So, I really like you but, y'know. People will see...

Waitaminute, are you not out?

Out? No, uh, I've got this job. A big job. I'm not sure I could ever... I mean with the job, y'know? Uh...

64

Uh-UH. I don't get involved anymore with guys who don't know what the fuck they are. Dammit.

Life's too short.

You're kinda cute. And funny.

But life's too fuckin' short.

RUMMAGE RUMMAGE

Carl found a ballpoint and scrawled his number on a book of matches.

Don't call me unless you're out. No closeted guys. Made myself a promise after the last freak show. So, later, funny Barney.

W-WAIT...

No—please don't go. Please don't go.

It was past 9 PM. There were still a few people on the Common trying to beat the humidity. He watched Carl recede into the park's shadows. Had he been the kind of guy who cried, that's what he would've done.

He'd fogged up his glasses, though, so he wiped them off, stood up, and went home.

And then he did what he always did.

Hiya, Shorty.

Yeah, hiya, Bahn.

At least since hitting puberty and discovering that sex and romance

were off-limits to him...

Hiya, fellahs.

Aintchoo never heard of Saturday??

Sheeeit.

He threw himself back into work.

How's the televised bowling, Mikey?

Yeah, 't's good, Bahn.

Longer days, more meetings, more brain power expended on solving the mayor's, the city's, the Commonwealth's problems...

...since I manifestly can't solve my own.

For starters, the Feds wanted to plow an extension of the interstate right through central Boston...

This just means leveling Chinatown, the Leather District, and sure, a chunk of the South End.

He and Transport Chief Fred Salvucci met with Bostonians at Little City Halls across town, and worked up alternative plans to preserve neighborhoods.

In cities across the country, community groups—like those organized by Jane Jacobs and many others in New York City—were pushing back against urban renewal.

GETTOUTTAH MY STREET, YOU KOOKY, GODDAMN BROAD!

BUZZ OFF, MR. MOSES!

And the mayor had him learn everything there was to know about encouraging financing, building, and managing affordable housing for low-income tenants. And how to make life a little better for the working adults, children, elderly, and disabled folks who lived there.

Boston's South End, 1968

NOS MUDAREMOS DE LA PARCELA 19

welcome to VILLA VICTORIA!

PARCEL 19

OUR PLAN

FAIR HOUS-ING

BRA & BHA?

How can I help?

He discovered something unfair if not surprising...

Listen, Harvard, maybe down at the Hall y'all think everyone here in the projects is a "successful" pimp or pusher. But t'aint actually the case, man. What about some JOBS, dig?

...very few tenants of Boston's Housing Authority were employed as members of its large work-force.

Jimmy, come look at this.

PAYROLL BOSTON HOUSING AUTHORITY 1968

Wouldn't tenants have a bigger stake in these buildings if they actually worked there as plumbers, carpenters, groundsmen, and managers?

Yeah, sure. But *who wouldn't* is Jake.

So, an idea was hatched. The mayor's office would take control of hiring at the Housing Authority, at least of summer maintenance workers, and make sure those jobs went to tenants.

Yeah, OK. **You tell Brier, though.** C'mon, I'm starved.

I'm carrying the mayor's coat today!

Barney wants to piss off Jake Brier, he can do it before **his own goddamn lunch.** Which one of you numskulls has my coat today?

Mr. Mayor, about that Civilian Review Board finding.

Later! Going to lunch!

Jake Brier was the longtime Boston Housing Authority boss—and used to having total control over all BHA jobs.

A Mistah Franks, from the mayah's office.

WHO?

And so that's what the mayor wants ta do.

ARE YOU FUCKIN' CRAZY??!

Excuse me?

Not you, Anita.

But look, Jake, don't you think the residents— sorry, mind if I smoke? It's lunch today...

Thanks. Dontcha think the residents would do a better job takin' care of these projects than the temps you've been hiring—who are they, anyway? Can't all be your relatives...

Look. What did you say your name is—Bernie? Look, Bernie, let me tell you how it is: these people the mayor wants to hire—

Residents.

Whatever you wanta call 'em, kid...

They ain't gonna do the grand spanking job you starry-eyed Ivy fuckin' Leaguers think they'll do. Get it through your thick fuckin' eggheads. They're NO GOOD.

If they were any fuckin' good, they wouldn't live in public housing in the first fuckin' place!

Tell Kevin: I ain't giving up my patronage jobs.

But Mr. Brier, dontcha think we'd have a better city if we—

BETTER FOR WHO?

He lost this first battle with the existing racist power structure, but there'd be others.

8. First Contact

One afternoon a nice-looking man showed up unannounced at the office, asking to speak to Barney.

Barney, some guy's here to see you. Says his name's John Smith.

I've seen you on TV. You seem like you give a damn.

Well, *the mayor* gives a damn. I just, y'know, help. So, what can I do for you, Mr. Smith?

Well, I'm, um, gay. And so are my friends. And we are just sick of getting harassed by th' cops at our neighborhood pubs in Bay Village.

Other than his bust of a thing with Carl, he'd never really met an openly gay man. So this was big. Also, outrageous.

Well, that shouldn't happen to anyone just trying to have a beer with friends in Boston!

CLIK.

Y'know, the more I'm told of incidents like these, in strictest confidence, of course, the better positioned I'll be to press the case with the police top brass.

He gingerly asked the man to set up a meeting with other victims.

But when the appointed day came, no one showed. Barney never saw the man again.

Uh, Polly, no word from Mr. Smith?

For the tenth time: NO!

That a new suit, boss?

He was surprised how sad he felt for the rest of the afternoon...

...really, for the rest of the week.

He seem a little mopey lately?

No, Your Honor.

Huh. OK. Carry on, Segel

But he pushed the loneliness away. Or tried to.

Weekends were the worst. To kill the time until life resumed again on Monday, he saw a lot of movies.

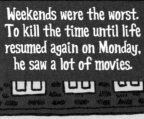

CINEMA 733

ELLIOTT GOULD HE LONG GOODBYE "

MARX BROS ROOM SERV

One Saturday night after a double feature, he was walking home, trying to pick some popcorn out of his teeth with a credit card.

There was a guy having a smoke. He mistook Barney's picking for a signal and fell into step behind.

Want company?

Huh? Oh, uh, OK.

It was his first time.

And it was a little surprising that it didn't feel more... momentous.

So, I usually charge $35, but I'll give you a deal. $30

70

Maybe it was different if you had feelings for the other guy?

Which clearly wasn't going to be the case tonight.

Oh! Sure. Lemme get my wallet.

But paying for it seemed an adequate solution for when being with someone became so urgent a need.

Oh shit, I've only got $19. Can I write you a check?

Nah. Just give me the $19 and we'll call it square.

So sometimes—not very often—he'd meet guys on the street or via the personal ads in the back of the alt weeklies and hook up.

And then three years had whizzed by. The idealism and passion of the '60s began giving way to the *Me Decade*.

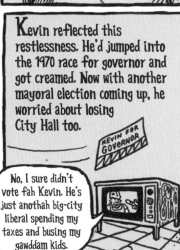

Kevin reflected this restlessness. He'd jumped into the 1970 race for governor and got creamed. Now with another mayoral election coming up, he worried about losing City Hall too.

KEVIN FOR GOVERNOR

No, I sure didn't vote fah Kevin. He's just anothah big-city liberal spending my taxes and busing my gawddam kids.

Where's the mayor? We're due at a community meeting in Jamaica Plain.

Left an hour ago. Said he was taking Kathy down the Cape overnight.

Which left Barney a lot less certain of their partnership...

I didn't raise you to do something you don't believe in.

I've been working my butt off for three years to build progressive government, not just Kevin's career. On the other hand, Mah, I dunno, this has been the opportunity of a lifetime.

Whose lifetime? His, maybe. You're just at the beginning of yours, Barney.

The Mayor thought Barney leaving his perch so close to power was ... nuts.

Who quits a job as chief of staff to Boston's mayor to go sit in a booger-y fuckin' carrel across the river as what, a grad student?

Dibs on his office.

No way.

But he knew his own mind. In mid-1971 he left City Hall to return to academia.

When're you and the mayor gonna do something about these lousy trains?

While a lot of flag-draped coffins were returning to America.

The Boston Globe

AMERICAN DEATHS IN VIETNAM SURPASS 45,000 PENTAGON REPORT

SGT. CALLEY MOVED TO HOUSE ARREST

TOP SECRET

His family was supportive (though they wondered how long he'd be able to stay away from politics).

Now I can finish my thesis.

Yes, okay. Great!

Not too long, as it turned out.

A focal point to sentiment against our involvement in Vietnam was a congressional race north of Boston where an antiwar lawyer named Mike Harrington was waging an underdog campaign.

VOTE PEACE!

When Harrington won in an upset, he looked around for a skilled political operator to run his new office in DC.

We've got to try and stop the bombings.

Later on you can write a thesis about how we ended the war.

He left his books behind. There were always new ones to read. No sense in carting around the ones he'd finished like precious gemstones.

Books, he thought, should be allowed to get on with their business of being read by as many people as they could lay their pages on.

He drove south all day, a patch of I-95 visible through a hole in the passenger-side floorboard.

Old Spice stick

newspapers

AM radio

Mound of shirts in need of dry cleaning

Fanta

Arriving in DC nine hours later, he almost stalled out on Thomas Circle before limping into a scary Sinclair to gas up, ahead of driving through tough-looking neighborhoods to the place he'd rented over the phone.

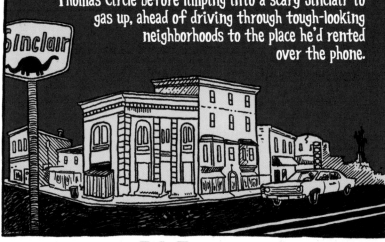

In DC, staffers follow a rigorous dress code; look nice, blend in.

Chunky horn-rims (30 years too early for them to be hip and ironic)

Not much of a haircut

Unbuttoned button-down

wrinkled

Converse high-tops (non-matching)

Boston Celtics Green laces

The landlord had sent a key. It worked, thank God, because he was no genius when it came to dodgy locks.

He fell asleep at once on the floor, exhausted.

Sock

PREVIOUS TENANT'S MAIL

ROACH

It was apparent to the staffers who met him the next morning that their new chief of staff wasn't cut from the same cloth...

So without futhah ado, let's welcome our new chief of staff.

9.
Punk
Staffer

The Capitol he arrived at was riven, like the rest of the country, by our brutal and pointless war in Vietnam.

HAWKS

DOVES

Harrington joined a congressional delegation divided by "the generation gap"—older Americans who backed our involvement in the war, and younger Americans demanding its end. Among the doves was Father Robert Drinan, one of the few Catholic priests ever elected to Congress.

His new boss didn't seem to expect Barney to play the part normally assigned staffers in the Kabuki theater that passes for social interaction on the Hill.

I'm having dinner with the majority whip. You want to come along? It should be fun.

Tip O'Neill? Is that kosher? You bringing staff to a members' dinner?

Look, I want to be surrounded by peers, not lackeys or sycophants.

Since boyhood, he'd admired men who moved nations at pen—rather than sword—point.

And he'd come to DC hoping to learn how great statesmen had passed heroic laws.

Hey, tomorrow let's schedule some time to plan our legislative strategy for the session...

Thaddeus Stevens

But Harrington had been elected promising to agitate...

...rather than legislate.

Actually, let's devote tomorrow to getting out my statement about the Pentagon's latest phony casualty stats.

Right around this time, Massachusetts filed suit challenging the legality of American troops in Vietnam, because Congress had never officially declared war.

But the federal court ruled that Congress had implicitly authorized the war by repeatedly voting to fund it.

Harrington had him work on efforts to turn off the federal funding spigot for combat in Asia...

My boss just thinks it is an amoral war.

Oh, well, *amoral.* Certainly not sure about **that.**

...but not enough members backed the effort, and the war ground tragically on.

Can we count on your support for the Boland Amendment?

Oh no. Tough vote. Don't wanna be seen as soft on the commies.

Still though, having an opportunity to do something about it was better than not.

OK, Congressman, thanks for your time. Let us know if you have any change of heart.

USELESS OLD FART. Someone should challenge him in the next primary.

As were new opportunities after work...

A bunch of us're headed over to the Hawk 'n' Dove after the vote. Come by!

Nice mention in the Boston paper. My boss says if I ever get quoted more than him, I'm fired.

...at dinners and watering holes where he began to make an impression on movers and shakers.

Nice to see ya, son. Naw, don't get up. Relax! Glad you could make it...

Nice work on th' Boland Amendment, by the way...

What he was realizing about DC was, he liked the platform and the place.

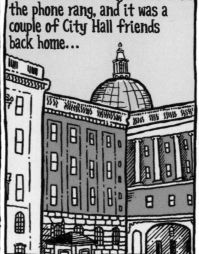

And he would've stayed. But then the phone rang, and it was a couple of City Hall friends back home...

...with news of a sudden vacancy in the state legislature.

Hey, Barn'– We're down at the *21st Amendment* having a few pops. Guess what we just heard...

The open seat was in the Back Bay neighborhood, where he'd lived while working for Kevin.

Seats like these don't grow on trees. You should run when you gotta chance.

Help you, Officer?

Note from your boss.

As he sat there after hanging up, he suddenly understood that he wanted to go for it.

Barney, congressman wants you to meet him on the South Lawn, then go with him to the floor.

He found the congressman outside with some visiting schoolkids.

Harrington, good-naturedly released him from his commitment to serve as chief of staff...

...though not without a hint of acid.

I don't think of you in that sort of leadership role. But what the hell, if you don't scratch that itch, it'll just keep itching. Besta luck.

He returned to his desk and dialed reporters back home to say he was jumping in...

LA BOSTON TOKYO

Goin' to Mass.?

You bet.

Sure, Barn, I'll run an item.

...and his sister Doris to ask her to pick up nominating papers at the election board so he could get on the ballot.

Kids, I'm running an errand for Uncle Barney. Back soon.

At Union Station, the cabbies glared in his direction for violating southern sleepiness as he ran to catch the overnight to Boston. His choice would have a lot of personal consequences. He'd use the train ride to try to get his head around them.

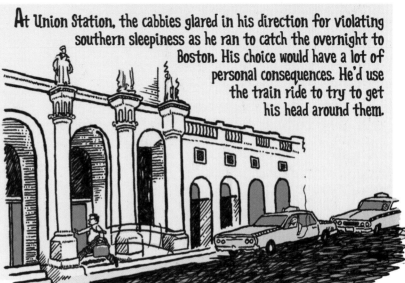

A day later, he stood out in front of Park Street station at 6:30 AM, trying to introduce himself to commuters and explain that he was a candidate for the legislature. Mostly they pushed past him, annoyed.

BOOK II

KING OF PIZZA
Boston Five Savings
TAXI

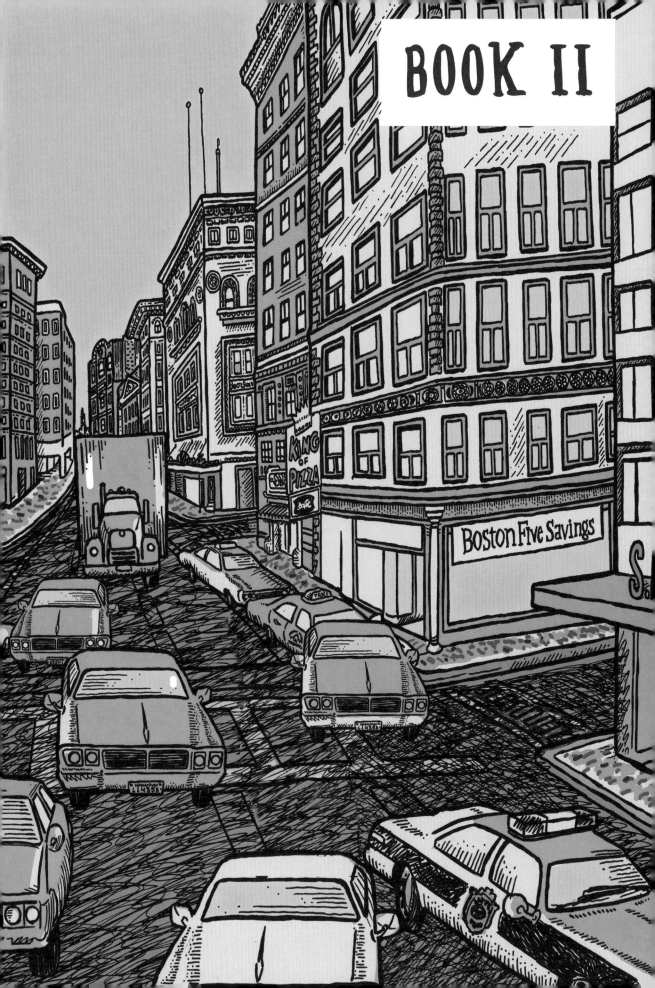

10.
Candidacy
DUNKIN' DONUTS
DUNKIN' DONUTS
DUNKIN' DONUTS
Hey, I know you! Where you been? Haven't seen you on the tube lately. The mayor's brains guy, right?
Been in DC, working for Congress.
Those snakes? What the hell for?
But I moved back. Runnin' for a seat at the State House.
Campaigning an hour. Already forgetting to smile.
Really? YOU?
Yeah. *ME.* You don't like the idea?
You don't look like a snake. You look like the guy who does the work for the snake.
Next!
I mean, look at those shoes. Ground down at the heels. You sure as hell aren't getting the cobbler vote.
Ta-da!
Florsheim
In fact, the staffers in Harrington's office had bought him a pair of new wing tips as a going-away gift, but they were still in his suitcase.
Oh wow! Thanks, guys.

On the other hand, a guy with crappy shoes might not rob us blind like all the other clowns.

An' snakes!

When's the vote?

September primary.

OK, I'll vote for you. HEY, BARKEEP, gimme a dozen lemon cremes. **Fresh baked.** Not the ones you pulled outta the oven last week.

November general.

Despite Boston's liberal reputation, cultural conservatism, Catholic orthodoxy, and white working-class resentment seethed.

And Democratic primaries had become proxies for cultural struggles happening across American society over Vietnam.

G@#!%

BOSTON WARD 5 DEMS TONIte 7 PM

BUMP

POW

BAM!

Also over divorce, women's lib, abortion, gays, ecology—you name it, Dems in 1972 were fighting over it.

In Ward 5, where Barney was a candidate, thousands of eighteen-year-olds were voting for the first time.

Oh, uh, hi. I'm Barney Frank, running for state rep.

Oh yeah? How d'you feel about amnesty?

I'm for it.

Ending rent control?

Against it.

Decriminalizing pot?

For it.

Mass transit?

Native Americans?

Beer on Sundays?

Like 'em all.

VOTE BARNEY for state rep

I'm thirsty. Up for the Rat?

Let's register to vote first. Dug that dude.

His friends thought there was no way he could lose.

How'd it go?

GREAT.

So-so.

VOTE BARNEY FOR REP.

district map

But if they saw him as an up-and-coming political talent, he saw himself as a fat Jewish guy from New Jersey who talked in a way that made some wonder if he had a speech impediment...

For the campaign, he'd camp out in his sister's spare bedroom.

...who was also a closeted gay man. If the first qualities didn't disqualify him from political life in Massachusetts, surely that last one would.

So on the train up to Boston he made himself a deal: he'd have a political life, not a personal one. But he wouldn't flinch from advocating for other people's gay rights.

THE POLITICS OF UPHEAVAL

SCHLESINGER JR.

That much he could do. And would do. But first, he had to win.

Where're you off to?

To greet commuters at the T.

At 5 AM on a Saturday?

Can't sleep.

VICTOR THEMO understands the needs of the old and the young.

Greetings, citizens!

So he ran like the underdog he felt himself to be, despite the fact that his opponents were a local oddball who lived with his mom and had maybe the worst campaign slogan ever...

...and a Republican grocer who may have been good for the district a generation earlier, but was too conservative for its voters now.

APPLE PIE & AIELLO for STATE REP!

With his family, Segel, and a small group of old friends from Harvard and City Hall, he knocked on doors,

OK. Don't crowd me, Ma.

Who's crowding? Knock already.

VOTE FRANK STATE REP.

stood with signs in the middle of busy intersections,

BARNEY

HONK IF YOU'LL VOTE BARNEY 4 STATE REP.

HONK

...every imaginable question.

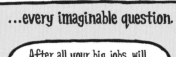

After all your big jobs, will you really care about local stuff? Storrow Drive hasn't been resurfaced in years. Our neighborhood is losing sleep over noisy cars, not B-1 bombers.

Look, if you elect me, I promise to fight potholes with the same tenacity in this job that I fought the Pentagon in the last one.

He wrote, xeroxed, and mailed position papers with the unshakable conviction that voters would actually read them...

...laboriously completing questionnaires from local, statewide, and national advocacy organizations,

Do you favor dog racing in the Commonwealth?

How about the SALT treaty on nuclear arms?

ERA?

Property Taxes?

Bombing Laos?

Handgun control?

including one envelope from a group calling itself "The Daughters of Bilitis"...

Ma, what's Bilitis? Is that what Aunt Fay had last year?

He called the Boston Public Library information desk, which was the kind of thing you did before the Internet.

Bilitis was the fictional female lover of the ancient Greek poetess Sappho, who lived on the Isle of Lesbos.

A chill ran up and down his spine, realizing he'd made contact with an actual gay organization in Boston.

OH! Uh, OK. Thanks for the info, ma'am.

Actually, the questionnaire tucked inside the envelope didn't leave much room for doubt about the type of group who sent it.

1. If elected will you immediately file legislation to abolish the Commonwealth's criminal sodomy laws, which have been on the books since not long after the Salem witch trials? Please respond: Yes or No answer (1 word limit)

2. If elected, will you take the earliest opportunity to file legislation to protect gay men and lesbians from being unfairly and baselessly fired by their employer simply because of their sexual orientation? Yes or No. No beating around the bush.

It was scary to publicly align himself with gay rights...

...but it was important to him to keep the bargain he'd made with himself. Although he might be afraid personally,

he would refuse to be scared politically.

Hey, Hamlet, you gonna mail your mysterious envelope or what? We're late.

His older sister.

So he checked the YES boxes and sent the questionnaire back.

ALL RIGHT, ANN, I'M COMING.

Hi! I'm calling to ask you to vote for Barney Frank!

Arthur Murray

FOR RENT

The pressures of the closet, combined with those of the campaign...

...meant he was no great pleasure to be around. Snappish with family, short-tempered with his friends, occasionally rude to a volunteer or even a prospective voter.

We've got a room full of people who've been licking envelopes and making calls for you all day. I'm gonna take them down to Harvard Gardens for pizza. Want to join us?

If I wanted pizza, I probably would've said, "I want pizza."

He was eating way too much junk food and ballooning in weight. But when election night came, and it was all over...

And in District 5, the winner for state representative is...

...despite not being cut from the conventional cloth for how a politician should look, act, sound (or love)...

Barney Frank, the smart, schleppy kid who used to run City Hall for Hizzoner.

...he won the fucking election. He couldn't quite believe it. It wasn't even close.

He didn't waste any time getting to work.

Gym bag briefcase

11.
State
House
Stories

In doing so he kept one thing in mind: it helps to know the rules.

Which way to the clerk's office, Trooper?

Closed though.

By studying the bylaws, he'd learned that state reps could only introduce legislation three times a year, and the first chance came in December.

Since being elected, he'd also learned that he was the ONLY candidate to say YES to the Daughters of Bilitis's survey.

He'd wound up meeting some of these women during the campaign and found their courage inspiring.

Barney, this is Elaine Noble. She's a professor at Emerson and is out and proud, baby.

Great.

Yeah. So, what's your deal, Barney?

Me? Oh, just supportive.

So he decided to make it his first official act, even before he got sworn in, to file the state's first-ever gay rights bill.

Newly elected representative, would like to file a bill.

A Bill

to prohibit discrimination in housing, insurance, employment, and public accommodation based on sexual orientation.

Oh happy day, a freshman filing a bill a month before he takes office...

Gotta problem with that?

HANDBOOK MASSACHUSETTS LEGISLATURE

Joint Rules of the Senate and House of Representatives... Session 169

Representatives duly elected, but not yet sworn in, may file legislation in December, prior to taking office in January.

Lemme see that damn thing.

Damned irregular. And that's before we get to the subject matter.

But you'll accept it?

Yeah. Best of luck, Mr. Frank.

You're gonna need it.

In January he finally took office (not literally, because incoming freshman reps were assigned communal space in the leaky State House basement). It didn't matter, though. He couldn't wait to get started.

Transportation was a big issue. Boston's proud, first-in-the-nation subway was a great engine for the region's economy. But suburban and rural areas of the state considered the T Boston's problem, and it was going broke.

If the city wants a subway, the city should pay fah it.

Phone call, Rep. Frank. It's City Hall.

Working with friends from the city's Transportation Department, he helped broker a compromise.

Might work.

Math adds up.

In return for suburban legislators supporting money for the T, Boston's reps would support the creation of regional buses to service the state's smaller towns, for the first time ever.

He earned a lot of chits with the State House grandees for getting the transport deal passed.

Oh! Mr. Speaker!

Now Representative, don't get up.

Careful of the drip, sir.

He was promoted to a seat on the Ways and Means Committee...

Anyhoo, came by to say nice work.

Bobby here'll show you your new office.

...which controls the state's spending. It was an unheard-of plum for a freshman representative.

In reality, the governor, speaker, and senate president made the decisions when it came to money.

But having a better office was cool.

Hey, Bahney, lunch?

Thanks, but gotta read this bill.

Read the summary, man. Who reads the whole bill?

Lunch?

Sure.

Frank can't come, he's readin' a bill.

RING RING

A *whole* bill?

Allard would call when passing through Boston. His national profile as a liberal activist was rising.

SOUTH STATION SNACK BAR

How's my favorite state legislator?

They'd have breakfast at the Ritz coffee shop, talking for hours about politics, policy, the problem with the Democrats (one per breakfast)...

Just coffee.

Ignore him, he'll have the eggs Benedict.

...and about the Refuseniks, the Weather Underground, the Israeli Labor Party, and how thrilled he was to be in the legislature. And how Al was thinking about going after a New York congressional seat.

Sometimes he showed up late, unexpectedly...

Surprise!

Last-minute meeting tomorrow at Brandeis. Couldn't find a hotel room this side of Stockbridge.

His first reaction was delight. It would be fun. Like a sleepover when he was a kid...

But just as quickly the physical (and emotional) logistics got in the way...

There's one bed, so you sleep there and I'll pull the chair and ottoman together.

Nonsense! You're not sleeping on a chair! We can share!

Uh, jeez. I want you to be comfortable, y'know?

I snore a little.

So what?

He was uncomfortable about Allard seeing him in his underwear, as he rushed around looking for his keys...

Hey, I'll sleep on the floor!

He felt more himself around Allard than he did around practically anyone—a scary proposition, one that he was in no way interested in testing.

Barn', easy, brother, I snore too...

No, really! You'll getta better sleep if I'm, uh...

...over at my sister's. Just a few blocks.

12. Fairer Shakes

WALLY'S

Mass Ave. at Columbus

If to be feelingly alive to the sufferings of my fellow-creatures... is to be a fanatic, I am one of the most incurable ever permitted to be at large.
—William Wilberforce

He believed that a purpose of democracy was to even the playing field so that everyone could access education, health care, economic opportunity, and political representation.

It's a racist goddamn town, Barney. You know as well as I. You've gotta single goddamn Black guy—Catholic, of course!—who's the only one you people have been willing to appoint to a board or a commission for, like, thirty years!

His friend Kay worked for the legislature's Black Caucus.

You people? What the fuck, Kay? You know how hard Kevin worked—shit— *I* worked to appoint—

Yeah, well, **work on this:** Why the hell don't we have a single Black person in the state senate, when there's enough Black folks in Massachusetts to make up at least two goddamn seats?!

Because the system's as rigged up here in the Northeast as it is down South. It just gets better PR.

That's right, Hackensack.

Bayonne.

Don't correct me when I'm agreeing with you.

Once a decade, state legislatures, following the national census, redraw political district lines to reflect a state's shifts in population.

If more people leave the city for the suburbs, for example, redistricting allocates the suburbs more representatives in Congress and the state house.

If there are more African Americans in a state now than there were ten years ago, then district lines should be redrawn to enable more political representation for African Americans.

But that's not the way it worked in Massachusetts in 1973 when the legislative bosses came up with a redistricting plan to quash Black hopes for a seat in the state senate.

Diminutive and dictatorial state senate president Billy Bulger wanted to keep just enough Black Bostonians in his district to scare away WHITE opponents.

Don't get any big ideas about running against me. We'll split the vote and elect a you-know-who.

When Barney agreed to fight for a Black state senate seat, the little senate president was pissed.

We'll talk to the **governor.**

CLINK

I Most Definitely DO NOT APPRECIATE this newly elected HAHVAHD loudmouth Goody Two Shoes *RADICAL* sticking his FATNOSE in the business of drawing the Commonwealth's Legislative Districts.

Some of Barney's fellow liberals refused to help, afraid of Bulger and his older brother Whitey, a one-man crime wave...

You're NUTS.

...responsible for much of the narcotics trafficking, numbers running, racketeering, bank robbery, and general thuggery going on between the Tobin Bridge and Providence, RI

BANG

For whatever reason, though, he wasn't easily intimidated...

ASSHOLES.

...by demagoguery.

These district lines are drawn to maintain neighborhood cohesion for the benefit of all Bay Staters.

These district lines have as much **cohesion** as the Austro-Hungarian Empire.

Or much else.

Should we call the cops?

Mighta been them who sent it.

When Bulger's boys rammed through a bill excluding more Black representation from the state senate, it was vetoed by the fair-minded Republican governor at the time.

Incensed, the bosses appealed to party loyalty and demanded that ALL Democrats vote to override the GOP governor's veto.

Turncoats!

To Barney, though, and the other liberals he'd helped persuade, it was a no-brainer...

I'll vote for a Republican plan ANY DAY OF THE WEEK, Mr. Speaker, before I vote for a RACIST one. Capisce?

There was a long impasse, but when the dust settled, he and his allies forced the legislature to create a seat in the state senate for an African American, a first for the state.

Fairer Shakes, Part Two

He wouldn't have the same kind of success with gay rights...

Surprisingly, when his bill to repeal the Commonwealth's criminalization of sodomy came to a vote, a majority seemed to be in favor.

Goodness gracious, the ayes have it.

The big electronic board near the speaker's podium displayed over two hundred little green lights— all signifying representatives voting with him.

Segel was a state rep now also.

He and his fellow liberals were astonished—thinking the house had just unceremoniously voted to decriminalize sex between same-sex partners...

Then, having had their bit of frat-boy fun, the hacks, ward heelers, and stooges changed their votes en masse to NO.

Oh wait, my mistake. It's the **nays** that have it after all!

Hey, Bahney, I heard your buttfuckin' bill went down to a resoundin' defeat.

Yeah, yeah. Gonna give me that coffee or what?

Which meant the sodomy statute, a relic from the Commonwealth's bad old witch-burning days, remained intact.

His response was to file a second gay rights bill.

You're just gonna keep doing this, aren'tcha?

My job? Yeah.

Please call my office as soon as you've assigned a bill number.

Yeah, yeah.

A bill to prohibit discrimination based on Sexual Preference in Housing, Employment, and Public Accomodations

At the bill's hearing, he was apprehensive when a young Black representative stood up to speak.

Ahem.

Many Black elders considered homosexuality a sin and wanted nothing to do with what they held to be an immoral gay rights movement.

ABOMINATION!

But he needn't have worried.

I've been dealing with job discrimination based on prejudice for a long time. And I think it's just as wrong when it's directed at gay people as I do when it's directed at Black people. Mr. Speaker, I support Representative Frank's bill.

EYES MISTING UP

His leadership started to get noticed. When LGBT Bostonians decided to hold a gay pride parade, they made him grand marshal.

GRAND MARSHAL

THANK YOU FOR SPONSORING GAY RIGHTS LEGISLATION STATE REP. BARNEY!!

He worried that his growing connection to gay lib would out him. But he couldn't ignore how nice it felt to be connected to the gay city, as if he was now in possession of a password revealing that the abandoned warehouse he'd been walking by for years was in fact a great house party.

GAY IS GOOD

REPEAL ANTI-GAY LAWS

PRIDE

HOW DARE YOU ASSUME I'M A HETEROSEXUAL

Thanks REP. FRANK

BETTER BLATANT than LATENT

It had only been a few short years from the day that gay man had showed up alone at his City Hall office complaining of police harassment.

Now here he was at a meeting at Arlington Street Church with dozens of confident-looking gay men and women...

...telling him they wanted not less but MORE policing at bars.

Thanks for coming, Rep. Frank. Since the riot in NYC, our own cops've sorta cut the old abuse shit. But now they just ignore us. We want them to do normal police stuff, y'know?

Stopping muggings.

Arresting pickpockets.

Sure, maybe our Boston cops had a change of heart. Or maybe they just don't wanna risk embarrassment by getting their asses kicked on Boston TV by a bunch of fit faggots, y'know? HAHAHA!

Probably makes sense to stop trash-talking them if you want their help.

I guess.

He offered to relay the community's concerns about safety...

First Precinct

BPD

...*and* privacy to the BPD.

So, look, Bahney, if one of your fags or lesbos comes in, an' they've been the victim of a mugging or robbery, as long as they'll ID the thug, I'll make it so's they can keep their own (pervy) ID anonymous. Sound good?

Yeah, sounds good, Captain. One more thing. Maybe you could try some respectful language, y'know? These people— they put up with a lot of abuse...

Oh, rest assured, we'll make every effort, when dealing with the gay community, to use the *Queen's* English.

BAHAHAHHAHHAH

Good one, Captain. **You** can rest assured my office'll be monitoring this.

A few of the gay bars in the Bay Village neighborhood attracted a rowdy, sometimes violent crowd that brought muggers, hustlers, pickpockets, and noise to the area. Some of the residents—many of them gay themselves— went to Barney because he was the only elected official who seemed to take their concerns seriously...

Any of you ever read this kids' book, *Fortunately*? I bought it for my niece. Well, your situation is a little like that book. Only in reverse...

Unfortunately, cracking down on rowdy bars is not something the state legislature can do anything about...

96

Oh...

Fortunately, City Hall *can* do something about it. We've gotta petition the Licensing Board to enforce an earlier closing time for the bars staying open until 5 AM.

The thing was, the owner of the worst-offending dive—a place called Jacques—was a notorious tough guy...

Get me everything there is to know about Barney Frank.

At a Licensing Board hearing, an attorney called Barney as a witness and asked him questions under oath about his connection to the neighborhood association's petition.

"Gosh, Representative, you're showing a lot of concern about the operations of a single insignificant tavern, albeit one with the distinction of catering to a mostly homosexual clientele. By the way, you aren't, homosexual, *I mean, are you?*"

The hearing officer quickly ruled the question out of order. But it hung in the air, frighteningly, and he heard himself answer:

No.

Lying about one's sexuality sucks. It sucked even more in 1974, when a lot of people did it more often than they do today.

But most people are never in a situation where they feel compelled to do it under oath.

RING

That REALLY SUCKED. It was humiliating and depressing, and for a few days after the hearing, he was so upset he had trouble getting out of bed.

RING RING

Hullo.

Barney, it's your mother.

I called your office. They said you weren't coming in today.

Yeah, Ma, feeling a little... uh, a little...

A little WHAT?

The hearing had been personally challenging. But the fact was, in the end, the Licensing Board voted to force the bars to close earlier. He'd won.

Down.

I'm coming over.

No, Ma, don't. I'm getting up. I'm going to work.

And his reputation for getting into the weeds of issues that impacted the quality of life of his constituents grew.

Here are those volumes you requested, Representative.

Thank you.

Something else?

Oh! No... well, to be honest, we don't get many legislators at the state library doing their own research. It's nice!

He wound up the go-to guy in the state capitol when it came to the regulation of sleazy businesses...

Look, if I represented Amish Country, I'd be looking up case law on horses and buggies.

CASE LAW ON PUBLIC MORALS

He worked to permit prostitution within an area downtown referred to by everyone, from sex workers to blue bloods, as the *Combat Zone*...

LIVE PUSSYCAT

Pilgri

...and to legalize at least some gambling. He thought of his aunts—hardworking Bayonne family women who'd take bus trips every three months down to Atlantic City to play the slots.

Rich folks could kick back at country clubs or summer homes, but for many, gambling was one of life's few pleasures. He thought it was elitist to deny their right to indulge it.

Just like he thought they had a right to adult entertainment in the Combat Zone, if that was their thing.

50¢ PEEP SHO

8MM FILMS
BOOKS
MAGS

RANDOM PATRON

When he introduced legislation to decriminalize possession of small amounts of marijuana,

Wait, WHAT??

...some of his colleagues just lost it...

MISTAH SPEAKAH!

If it's not prostitution, if it's not fornification, if it's not support for the rights of the Homos, then it's legalizing dope. When, in the name of all that is holy, is the gentleman from Back Bay gonna stop? WHEN?? WHEN??

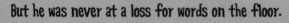

But he was never at a loss for words on the floor.

Mr. Speaker, it's true that I've introduced bills related to pornography, gambling, prostitution, adultery, homosexuality, and now, marijuana. But I will make this commitment to my colleague: I'll keep trying until I find **something** that he likes to do.

Which made him something of a hero to the gang in the press gallery.

That Barney kills me!

GLOBE   UPI

HERALD

Still, by his fourth term, he was feeling stuck and demoralized...

Somethin' botherin' you?

No.

I might not see, Representative,

but I ain't blind.

You gonna give me my coffee or what?

He fell out with his old boss when Kevin became more interested in building a new political machine than fighting for better government.

And the new governor, Mike Dukakis, was cutting spending on social services in a way Barney felt no Democrat should.

Plus, he'd infuriated fellow Dems by again breaking party ranks and endorsing a Republican for reelection to the US Senate. Edward Brooke was the Senate's lone Black member—and a man of integrity and grace. Barney felt the Senate needed more, not less, Black representation.

But you didn't buck the Democratic establishment without paying a price. A new speaker was hell-bent on making Barney pay it.

Gimme a plan to block all Barney's bills.

An' hey! Let's screw with his committee assignments!

That's the stuff!

CONTEMPLATION of CAMPAIGNING in WESTERN MASSACHUSETTS

He seemed unlikely to move up. Too liberal, too Jewish, too Jersey to get elected statewide. He'd managed to attend Harvard Law during his off-hours and had done well, but not because he ever wanted to practice law. He just wanted to author better bills.

And the most obvious fit for a congressional seat—the district with Cambridge at its center—was held by Tip O'Neill, God bless him, who wasn't going anywhere.

Hiya, Tip!

Howaya, fellahs!

But the truth was that his depression was about loneliness, not politics. He'd broken things off with a nice woman whom he'd dated a few times in a half-hearted attempt to be something (straight) that he wasn't.

That went badly.

Now that he actually knew some gay people, he saw that many were building seemingly happy lives. He wondered why he couldn't figure out how to do the same.

He understood that coming out, at least to his closest friends, was the place to start.

So that's how it is, Segel.

Jeez, Barn. No problemo here, obviously, but maybe better to, y'know, keep it quiet.

Friendly's

Though they couldn't help but worry...

So that's how it is, Joe.

New friend Joe also happened to be gay. He liked to hang out in the State House visitors' gallery, listening to the floor debates.

...about the potential risk to his political career...

Be careful

and discreet.

I gotta go to th' john. Don't tell anyone about this while I'm gone.

His siblings were supportive, but had their own worries, too.

Look, maybe don't tell Mom.

Gotta boyfriend?

I wish.

He was forty years old as the 1970s limped to a close. The sourness he felt personally was mirrored by what was occurring beyond the borders of his own life.

Vote Barney
Neatness isn't Everything

Ted Kennedy's campaign for president, which Barney had enthusiastically supported, had been a bust.

Um, my brothahs... and so on...

Ronald Reagan and the Moral Majority were politically ascendant...

Welfare queens are at this very minute using government benefits to dine on filet mignon at the Waldorf.

...that lunatic ayatollah glared from every newspaper, magazine, and TV screen.

And in March, he received a shattering phone call. Allard had been murdered at his law office by an unstable ex-student.

101

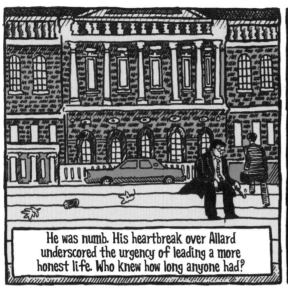

But if he left politics to come out, then what? How would he make a living? Teach? He'd never finished the damn thesis. Public interest law? Talk radio?

And then, a different phone rang. This time, the call wasn't local...

He was numb. His heartbreak over Allard underscored the urgency of leading a more honest life. Who knew how long anyone had?

...and it wasn't for Barney. It was for Father Drinan, the liberal priest who represented suburban Boston in Congress.

13.
ROMA
CALLING

There have been times when things that were happening half a world away at Vatican City had more impact on Boston than whatever was going on in Harvard Yard or atop Beacon Hill.

May 1980 was one of them.

The Holy Father says, "My son, you may serve God, or you may serve the Americans in their Congress, but you may not serve both."

I understand.

The world had grown accustomed during the twentieth century to elderly Italians on the throne of St. Peter...

...mumbling conservative or sometimes more liberal niceties about world peace and eradicating poverty and hunger...

...while going about the business of managing their global corporation. Direct papal intrusion in American politics was unusual.

But then, so was everything else about the new pontiff who burst onto the world stage in 1978 after the weirdly murky death of his predecessor.

White smoke from the Vatican chimney means a new pope has been elected.

Handsome, virile, and defiance personified when it came to the communists ruling his native Poland, Pope John Paul II was a rock star.

And he toured like one, holding huge outdoor masses in American cities soon after his elevation.

Including in Boston, where he was welcomed by the archbishop, Cardinal Humberto Medeiros.

The cardinal had grown up an hour south, in Fall River, Massachusetts—where textile mills had once provided stable employment for Portuguese immigrants like Humberto's parents.

No smoke means shuttered factories and hard times.

But after World War II, the mills began to fail or move south to states without labor protections.

Perhaps as a result, the cardinal had developed a pretty fatalistic view of the things his parishioners could expect from this life. A woman's right to choose wasn't one of them, and in this, he was very much in sync with the new pope.

At a supper held after John Paul II's huge mass on Boston Common, Humberto just might have leaned over and mentioned offhandedly...

You know, Holy Father, one of our priests here troubles me. He serves in the Congress in Washington, where he supports the sacrilege of allowing females to terminate the lives of their unborn babies.

Co! Mowisz powaznie?!*

*"Are you shitting me?!" in Polish

A few weeks later, on a Saturday afternoon in May, Jimmy Segel's wife, Mimi, caught wind of the shocking news that Father Drinan would be forced to leave Congress.

Oh, hey, Mimi! Listen, gotta sec? Well, I just heard the most surprising rumor over at Saint Ignatius. Really, I'm just floored!

Coolidge Corner, Brookline

Jimmy was taking the kids to a matinee. Mimi decided it couldn't wait.

Barney? Hi, it's Mimi. Honey, are you sitting down?

YOU'RE SHITTING ME!

He admired Father Drinan unreservedly.

WOW.

After a decade in Congress, Drinan had become one of the nation's most influential liberals, earning himself, among other accolades, a prime spot on Nixon's enemies list.

For fuck's sake, will no one rid me of this turbulent priest?

Yessir.

Workin' on it.

But the father's forced retirement represented a rare opportunity to advance—and with the deadline to file congressional candidacies only days away, there was no time to do anything but hustle.

Where're you rushing off to, hon?

Washington, I hope.

DeLuca's

The first problem was his address. Barney's apartment was in Boston's Back Bay, about a mile outside Drinan's district. So the next weekend, he moved.

BOSTON

SUBURBS

NEWTON CENTRE INBOUND

On the other hand, he had good name recognition from Boston media. Voters perceived him as smart and mostly liberal. Like them.

Meet Barney Frank! For Congress!

UH. HELLO. I'M BARNEY

They also thought he was honest.

BARNEY FRANK. RUNNIN' FOR CONGRESS.

As wicked schleppy as that guy is, you figure he ain't skimmin' from the till, y'know?

Totally!

His sister Doris rented a little campaign office. People began to wander in: union folks, academics, part-time working moms, students…

ELECT BARNEY FRANK to U.S. CONGRESS

...and a tall, freckled high school senior named Conan O'Brien, who helped out all summer long before destiny took him to Hollywood.

But grassroots enthusiasm didn't mean he was a shoo-in. At least six other candidates jumped into the race.

Some of the liberals bitterly resented Barney's parachuting into the district solely for the purpose of running for Congress.

And then there was the possibility of John Kerry's candidacy. At the time, he was a decorated combat vet who had returned from Vietnam to electrify the nation by questioning the war in a televised hearing:

Senator, how do you ask another man to be the last man to die for a mistake?

Kerry reminded people of JFK. He would've made a strong candidate. But in the end he passed, worried that if he ran the liberals would split the vote...

If I ran for Senate instead, would you support me?

Absofuckinlutely.

...and throw the race to a conservative Democrat named Arthur Clark, the mayor of Waltham, a small city west of Boston, and popular owner of a tire dealership.

VOTE CLARK

CLARK

Lemme say a word about subway funding.

And then I'll talk about the MX missile.

Donors, party elders like Drinan, and local powerbrokers, gravitated toward Barney.

Eventually, the other liberals dropped out and endorsed him—which left a one-on-one matchup with Clark, who took to the airwaves with attack ads.

My friends, the 4th District needs a congressman who'll champion small-town New England values, and those don't include PORNO, POT, or PROSTITUTION.

Clark opposed abortion. Barney pointed out that many of the same folks who were so fervently pro-life were also opposed to food stamps and welfare.

I guess they believe life begins at conception and ends at birth.

Just days before the primary, His Eminence weighed in. Having helped engineer the infuriating lefty priest's ouster, the idea that he might be replaced by

this slobby Jew, this promoter of all manner of venality, well, that was just intolerable.

These are blood-drenched times.

So he wrote to every Catholic voter in the district to make damn sure it didn't happen.

It is a sin for a Catholic to vote for any candidate who supports abortion. Period.

Make certain the newspapers print this.

Of course, Eminence.

Humberto's letter put Barney on the defensive at first...

Your fat boyfriend's screwed now. Har!

Maybe...

Within days, though, sentiment swung the other way.

Hey, I'm a good Catholic, but maybe the Church oughta concern itself with what's going on under its own skirts, if you get my meanin'.

EXACTLY

No one anticipated celebrating early. And they were right.

Primary election night arrived. They sat nervously in a suburban hotel suite watching the returns...

Don't chew your nails, Barney. Please.

But by midnight, the returns were in. Although he'd only edged Clark by a few points, he'd won the Democratic nomination for Congress.

They passed out champagne. He would've loved a cigar but hadn't brought one. (That was the sort of thing a spouse might remember, he thought, if a guy had one.)

Sometimes in Massachusetts, winning the Democratic primary is tantamount to being elected. But 1980 was different. The Church's hostility and Mayor Clark's near miss indicated a tough race in November.

Western end of the district's a bitch, boss.

Yeah.

And President Carter's weakness at the national level—the energy crisis, inflation, and the failed mission to rescue American hostages in Tehran—didn't help…

Luckily, Barney's Republican opponent was a right-wing dentist no one had ever heard of named Richard Jones…

You think we should worry?

Not unless he changes his name to Shirley.

Dr. Jones wasn't exactly in step with the average Massachusetts voter.

For starters, he was a member of the notorious John Birch Society…

Oh, hello.

Unlike, say, Klansmen, you don't really know Birchers are royal nutjobs by their appearance. You have to wait until they open their mouths…

That's why fluoride in our water supply is a pinko plot to corrupt the purity of our essence. BUT fluoride's not the only thing that's bad! THE BLACKS and the JEWS and the CATHOLICS are bad too!

Which Dr. Jones did. With abandon.

Speaking of Jews, Barney Frank wants your children to smoke pot. He wants hookers to work your streets. He wants your menfolk to blow their paychecks on booze.

And... he's from New Jersey!

Do we ignore him because he's a right-wing gadfly with no money or visibility, and run out the clock? Or do we respond and elevate his name recognition?

Let's go after the fucker.

Agree with Dottie.

MA. 4TH C.D.

FRANK

Can you imagine the people of Massachusetts sending a member of the John Birch Society to Congress?

That's right, this Republican was an active Bircher. So if you run into him, tell him this is Massachusetts, not Texas, and that...

...around here we support Barney Frank!

CANDY NECKLACE

THUMB TACS

JOKE FANGS

OOOH SCARY!

BLAH BLAH

Gbbrrr

UHF VHF OUTER SPACE

The stress of the final leg of the campaign—the thought that he could blow what would probably be his only shot at a seat in Congress because of an unprecedented right-wing wave—was tremendous. It showed on the candidate, and it wasn't pretty.

Ma'am, thank you for saying you'll vote for me. Though I find your saying that you also plan on voting for John B. Anderson for president...

...particularly idiotic!

I like that Bahney, he's so full of piss 'n' vinegah.

I LIKE THAT BAHNEY.

WHAT?

Oh yes.

Who wrote our press release on inflation?
I did.
It says "federal **monies.**" Never say "monies." Who says "monies"? **NO ONE**, that's who!
OK, Barn.
Staff and volunteers fought hard for him because they wanted a person as talented and smart as him to represent them in Congress...
grumble
STOMP
STOMP
...but that didn't make him a delight to be around.
Could I borrow $20? I need some monies to go buy a gun and shoot myself.
SLAM
Volunteers drove him so he could prep on the way to events.
Now, look, he's brilliant. And we love him. But he's also the most insufferable backseat driver on the planet. Don't let him make you cry.
FRANK
VOTE
Dottie had been Father Drinan's staff director. Now she was helping Barney.
CRY? Yeah. Not happening, Mrs. Pynchon.
A Day Later
YOU JUST TOOK THE **WRONG EXIT!** YOU SWITCHED INTO THE CENTER LANE FOR **ABSOLUTELY NO REASON!** PLEASE. **PLEASE.** PAY ATTENTION! HURRY UP! THERE'S NO POLICE IN THIS STRETCH. **FLOOR IT!**

Election night finally arrived. They huddled in another suburban hotel suite, watching the returns. The news from across the nation was grim.

The over-the-hill, cowboy-actor reactionary had swept the presidency in a landslide.

Social conservatives like Moral Majority founder Jerry Falwell and anti-women's-rights wicked witch Phyllis Schlafly were all over the airwaves crowing about a scary new American dawn.

During the campaign, Jimmy Segel had said:

You gotta love Barney Frank to like him.

And at the end of the night it seemed that just enough voters of Massachusetts's 4th Congressional District agreed.

The thing about New Englanders is, for the most part, they can skip the glad-handers and the sweet talkers. Neither gruffness nor outright grouchiness is apt to scare them off.

I'll have the **chops**. Oh wait! I'll have the **baby back ribs**. NO! I'll have the **prime rib**. Hold on, I'll—

You'll have broken ribs if you don't hurry it up 'n' order.

DURGIN-PARK

Oh, hi! We're looking for the road to Sunday River.

Can't get theyah from heyah.

HA! Good one!

Which may be part of the reason why, when the last precincts reported, it was close—a margin of just 4%—but in fact, he'd been elected.

FRANK WINS

Wow!

US GOVERNMENT
G1935

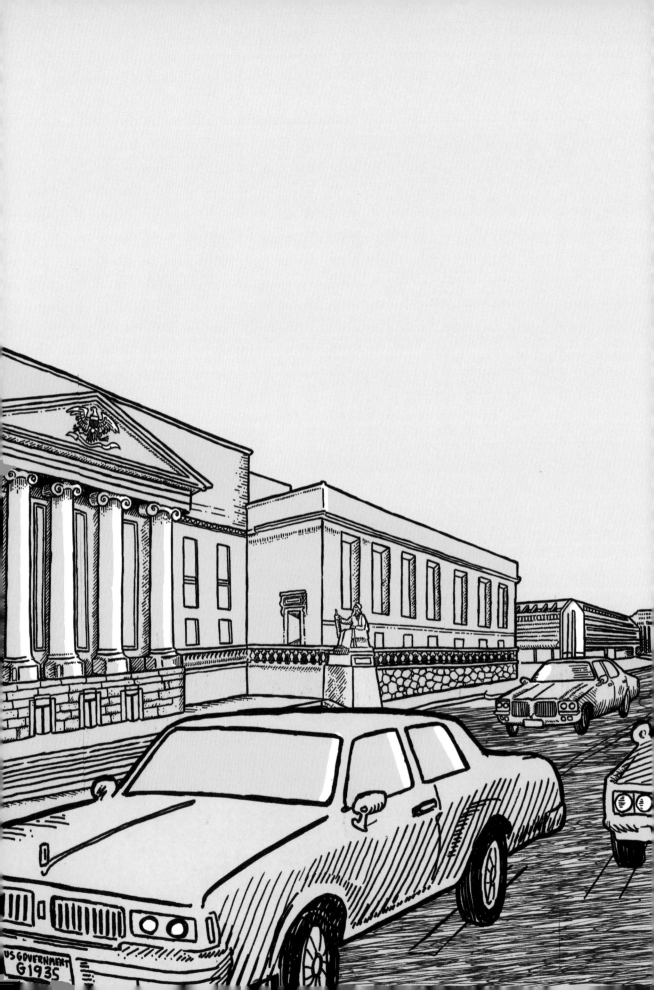

BOOK III

In a town with two castes...

Principals

Staffers

...it was nice to return to DC with a ticket for the Grown-Ups Table.

May I help you?

Barney Frank. Newly elected.

Of course, Representative. We have your member pin right here.

Not that anyone would mistake his new apartment for being very adult.

Hellooo? Anyone home? Barn?

It looked like a student crash pad. Not that he cared, having no intention of doing much of anything here except sleeping and gulping down a cup of coffee in the morning before hustling to work.

Hey, Joe, great to see you. Any trouble finding the place?

Just the last thirty seconds. What's with all the Hefty bags taped to the windows?

DIY curtains!

He was clear about his approach to the new job. He intended to legislate. First step: mastering federal law governing things he cared about...

...social justice, consumer rights, affordable housing,

Doug, Peter, get me the regs for the rental housing voucher program. Same for home heating assistance and school lunches.

and the parliamentary tactics he'd need to advance them.

Maybe not gonna be an "Oh, What a Beautiful Mornin'" sorta office culture...

115

True, it was a lousy time to be a liberal entering Congress.

With POTUS slashing infrastructure, school lunches, and environmental protection to pay for his fat-cat tax cut and ginormous Pentagon spending spree.

Barney impressed Speaker O'Neill as a quick study and an even quicker tongue. He was often tapped to lead the counterattack.

We don't begrudge President Reagan the occasional nap. It's what he does when he's awake that bothers us.

He won a coveted seat on the Judiciary Committee, where some of the hottest-button issues—criminal justice, policing, civil rights, and impeachment—are debated.

That's why it's critical, Mr. Chairman, that we save the Legal Services Corporation. So that poor **people have some way to fight** unfair evictions, or eminent domain that lets the state take whatever it damn well pleases.

Hogwash!

Shaddup!

BRAVO!

Gruff and impatient as he could be, being around all these pols, even the insipid, venal, or lazy ones, brought out his more collegial side...

Representative, gotta sec?

Which was a good quality to have when the goal was always to convince a majority of people to vote with you, rather than against you.

He enjoyed their stories, identified with their insecurities, liked sharing a brownie with them in the cafeteria,

Out of bean soup again, Congressman!

Sorry, Congressman.

I'll get the Congressman's soda and brownie.

OK, Congressman.

commiserating about the ribbon cutting or town hall they had to do this Saturday, or next Saturday, or on an endless string of Saturdays until they lost reelection or dropped dead.

Yeah, you guys really got it rough. Try being the goddamn delegate from Guam.

As people, he just sorta liked other members of the House, even many of the Republicans.

14. FAULT LINE

Among its other responsibilities, the Judiciary Committee oversaw women's rights to reproductive health services—including abortion—as established by the US Supreme Court in *Roe v. Wade*.

Ugh.

Justice Harry Blackmun wrote the decision.

A coalition of evangelical Christians and conservative Catholics in Congress were proposing a constitutional amendment banning abortion.

STOP ABORTION NOW

Speaker O'Neill was a devout man, and anguished by abortion. But he also felt that recriminalizing it would send poor women back to the butchers and quacks of his youth.

The Boston Post
MOLASSES TANK EXPLOSION

So he took Barney to lunch.

Look, Bahney, I need you to use all your parliamentary skills to keep this piece of s-h-i-t amendment away from the floor.

G-u-l-p

For a freshman member who'd just won his seat by barely defeating right-to-lifers, this was no plum assignment.

I know you have a lotta faith in open debate, son, but abortion'll split our Dem caucus at a time when we need unity.

But the Speaker wasn't a guy that a guy said no to.

OK, Mr. Speaker. I'll make sure the amendment stays bottled up in a subcommittee.

Attaboy.

C'mon in for a sec—I'll give ya one of these *bee-u-ti-ful* Cohibas I got from the Canadian ambassador.

AHEM.

Tarnation.

No! Those AWACS radar planes absolutely mustn't be sold to the Saudis!

Outrageously pretending not to notice waiting cardinal because deep in conversation.

Sir, is Cardinal Medeiros in the habit of showing up unannounced?

No, he certainly is not. No doubt he's here to roast me over the hellfires for stalling the abortion amendment I just secretly told you to kill.

Should I say a prayer for you on my way back to the office?

Yeah. The hard stuff. Old Testament. Think I'll need it.

>Sigh<

Please ask the cardinal in.

Your Eminence! Now this is a heavenly surprise! To what do I owe the unalloyed pleasure?

I have a bone to pick with you, Speaker.

It despairs me to hear so, Your Eminence. *Pray tell*, what about?

As you are no doubt aware, Speaker, an earthquake hit the **Azores** several months ago and work on an emergency aid package has, I am distressingly told, barely commenced.

Wait...what? He's talking about *disaster relief*? Not abortion?

Sorry, Eminence, the earthquake in the...?

In the Portuguese AZORES, Mr. Speaker.

I see. Hmm. Barely commenced, you say?

Well, that's perfectly outrageous!

Send Chris and Ari in here.

ON THE DOUBLE.

EMINENCE.

Enough chitchat, gentlemen. The cardinal has traveled all the way from our fair city to learn firsthand, from both of you, about your progress in putting together the RAERP.

The, ah, RAERP, sir?

That's right, Weiss, the Rapid Azorean Earthquake Relief Package—the RAERP. Are we not feeding you boys enough? Blood sugar low? We talked about it just last week.
But, sir—
Making this up as he goes along
Feigning exasperation
No BUTS about it, Matthews! The United States Congress is delighted to come to the assistance of our Azorean brothers and sisters suffering with the threat of, er, cholera!
There is a threat of cholera, Eminence? Well, there you go, Matthews! With the cholera and the structural damage, the loss of the electric grid...
You DO appreciate the need to expedite here, boys? None of your legislative doodling and dawdling! By the way, Your Grace...
...what figure do you imagine might best set our Azorean friends back on their path of industry and initiative?
AH. Cough. Well...
$50 million
Fine, fine, let's go ahead and make it **$60 million,** in honor of the special bond we have with the Azorean people.

Thank you, my son. There are other matters to discuss, but not today.

Fine. Fine. Great to see you.

Boys, go find me sixty large.

On it.

Don't lose your notes.

No, Your Grace.

15.
The
American
(Pipe)
Dream

Barney was also assigned a seat on the Banking Committee, which oversaw mortgages, and, by extension, housing.

After World War II, the federal government offered developers big loans to build new apartment blocks, on the condition that they charge affordable rents for a period of about forty years.

But by the '80s, many of these agreements were expiring. And the suburban ideal of the 1950s was fraying. Cities were once again desirable to young professionals.

Defunct Suburban Mall

★ma y's

URBAN CORE HIPSTER APARTMENT BUILDING   LATTES   BIKES

Landlords, anxious to cash in, were harassing low-income and elderly tenants to leave...

WATER OFF BETWEEN 9-5 TOMORROW —MGMT

ELEVATOR OUT OF SERVICE ALL WEEK —MGMT

...or simply evicting them altogether...

...then rehabbing the vacant apartments and renting them to waves of Yuppies hitting the cities in an ever-rising tide of gentrification.

With the help of housing advocacy groups and allies in Congress, Barney pushed hard for a federal answer to the problem—like a low-income tax credit to incentivize developers to construct new affordable apartments.

Here in DC, satisfaction with his professional life began, for the first time ever, to spill over into his personal life.

Dunno, Barney. You sure this's a good idea?

This? This what?

This *this*. You having a drink in a gay bar.

Oh, I think these guys'd be discreet, don't you?

Maybe take some pride that someone who may be one of their own is getting a little positive notice...

Maybe. Or maybe jealous of that fact.

Don't be so trusting. Just because a guy's gay doesn't mean he can't be an asshole.

Jeez, Joe, lighten up. We're at a bar. We're having a nice time. Cute guys are walking by us, smiling.

Yeah, sorry, you're right. Really, Barney, you had a kick-ass first term. Here's to even bigger and better things in your second.

CLINK

Hi, Congressman. Saw that article about you in *U.S. News*—Best Freshman. CONGRATS!

But given the goings-on up on Beacon Hill a few weeks later, it suddenly looked like there might not be a second term.

Send in a page.

Yes, sir.

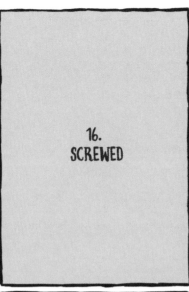

16.
SCREWED

The 1980 census showed that Massachusetts's population was down, and the state had to lose one seat in Congress.

Overnight this to DC.

NEW DISTRICT MAP

State Senate President Billy Bulger was bent on avenging Barney's work several years back to create that Black senate district.

Right away, Senator Bulger.

And he had the help of a new right-wing governor and a new state house speaker, neither of whom had any use for Barney's brand of...

Bleeding-heart pinko leftyism.

So they drew the new district lines with one goal in mind: screwing Barney by combining his district with the adjoining one, represented by the state's only congresswoman.

SHIT.

Who they figured would slaughter him in a head-to-head matchup.

Inexhaustible, successful, impeccable Margaret Heckler, from upscale Wellesley, Mass., was popular with her constituents.

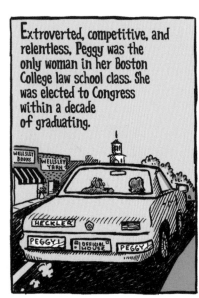

Extroverted, competitive, and relentless, Peggy was the only woman in her Boston College law school class. She was elected to Congress within a decade of graduating.

A suburban soccer mom long before that phrase entered America's political lexicon, she maintained a carefully moderated voting record so as never to find herself out on a limb.

She was regularly photographed in every conceivable district setting: parades, graduations, canned-goods drives, ribbon cuttings, turkey giveaways, nor'easter damage inspections (for those, the grin was swapped out for a look of studied concern).

Welcome, Congresswoman!

WELL, HI THERE!

Peggy focused on constituent services (helping people qualify for disability benefits or expediting their passports, that sort of thing) and on getting reelected, rather than on policy or governing. The voters liked her and took pride in sending one of the few Republican women to Congress.

She wasn't happy about running against Barney. His sarcasm and unkemptness bugged her. But she was confident that she'd win.

OK, what's next?

Serving as the honorary judge of a figure-skating tourney in Sherborn.

Got my skates?

In the trunk.

Barney, on the other hand, was anything but confident.

The new district map was the political equivalent of brain cancer. The prognosis sucked.

Maybe I shouldn't run.

Umzin!

The first reelction strategy session was depressing.

Since college, his home base had been metro Boston. But now he'd been handed a district where the largest city was Fall River, which wasn't metro anywhere.

But it was a place where Peggy Heckler was a known quantity. She'd been careful throughout her career to support safety net programs that the small city depended on.

Don't forget your roll!

Having this put-together lady from Wellesley as its voice in Congress gave downtrodden Fall River a touch of class.

What's next?

SOUP KITCHEN

Anti-litter event in Dover.

But now, the dynamic that had her easily winning year after year had changed. She'd caved to pressure from the president and voted for his budget cuts...

So get out there and win one for the Gipper, Penny!

Her shift to the right gave Barney the opening and the jolt of energy he needed.

Many people won't be able to heat their homes this winter because Ronald Reagan says he needs to help the oil companies, and Margaret Heckler says she needs to help Ronald Reagan.

I'd like to hear less about **supply side**, and more about **home** economics.

Mark Sullivan was the director of Citizens for Citizens, a social services organization and the closest thing Fall River had to a political boss.

What'd ya think, Marky?

Talks too fast, but he makes a lotta sense...

I'm just here for the free chow.

I'm liking him.

He and his union allies had supported Peg for years. But now they felt betrayed. Her embrace of Reaganomics meant they hadn't left her—because she'd already left them.

125

And the thing about Barney that began to shine through was that he identified more with places like Fall River than his fancy Harvard pedigree suggested. People who were hurting saw past his curtness and recognized his compassion.

How long were you over there?

Almost two years, man. But part of me's *still* way the fuck over there.

Gimme your number. I'll call the VA.

No "Thank you for your service" bullshit. Weird.

Yeah. Just "Give me your number. I'll call the friggin' VA."

Sorta liked him.

Whereas Peggy was increasingly coming off as sorta phony.

Now there's three good-lookin' fellahs who I bet would each love an American flag lapel pin!

126

By September he'd pulled even in the polls—especially after a few debates where Heckler's justifications for slashing the home heating program fell on pretty deaf ears.

So she went negative.

BEFORE YOU VOTE ON NOVEMBER 2, COMPARE THE CANDIDATES

MRS. HECKLER
Family Woman
Neat as a Pin

FRANK
Likes Porn
Hairy Nostrils
From Joisey

She'd never been a very subtle pol, and now all those stagy pictures of her smiling while judging spelling bees and pouring syrup at pancake suppers...

...seemed at odds with the desperate negativity of her TV commercials.

PORNOGRAPHY
POT
PROSTITUTION
PERVERSION

Barney's team, led by Boston ad men Martilla & Kiley, volleyed with their own commercial that riffed off his having been named Freshman Member of Congress Rookie of the Year.

The spot showed real footage of him powering a hit at a softball game, then speeding his bulk around the bases and sliding into home, with a voiceover of his accomplishments in Congress.

It caught people's attention—showed him as a guy they could relate to. Not some Harvard egghead or Brookline snob.

Hey, I'm voting for that fat guy!

His second ad was even more effective...

I just retired, and I'm looking forward to my social security. In fact, I'm **depending** on it. So all this talk about cutting social security is making me nervous. That's why I'm glad Barney Frank's in Congress...

Barney helped stop the Republicans from cutting cost-of-living and Medicare benefits. And he'll keep fighting to protect our social security. How can I be so sure that Barney'll do right by us older people? Because he's my son.

Me too!

The ad turned Barney's mom, Elsie, into a sought-after celebrity on the campaign trail—especially at nursing homes and senior centers.

They keep us doped up in here. Will you tell your son?

I'll do more than that!

Mr. Souza, such the kidder! Heh heh.

Soon she became a power in her own right at the Massachusetts Elder Caucus, a fearsome advocacy group.

GOVERNOR'S OFFICE

Charge!

It was becoming clear that Barney would win Newton and Brookline, and Peg would take Wellesley and the string of more conservative towns to the south. That left Fall River as the main battleground.

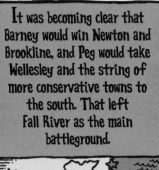

MASSACHUSETTS

CT RI.

Her operatives amped up a whispering campaign down there about Barney's personal life.

Just sayin'. Forty-two-year-old guy, single. Big into homo rights? C'maaaan...

BEER COKE HIGHLAND SPA HOOD MILK

By this point, Markey Sullivan had already endorsed Barney. He wanted to know what his get-out-the-vote folks would be up against in the campaign's final days...

Look, chief, I dont care who you you sleep with. It doesn't matter for how you do your job, which you do damn well.

SCRATCH SCRATCH

I only want to know what I'm dealing with, so I know how to win. To beat Peggy. So I'm askin', this rumor, is it true? Are you gay?

HIGH SPA

It made him almost physically ill, but he rationalized that the only person he hurt by not telling the truth was himself.

Uh, no, Mark.

The calendar barreled toward Election Day. He was hard on himself and harder on everyone else.

There's no phone number on this message!

Its from your sister. I assumed—

TEAM BAR

NO! DON'T ASSUME!

One volunteer, tired of being yelled at by a candidate she admired hugely but was also growing hugely sick of, began secretly calling him the Congressmonster.

The nickname stuck.

Sure, Barney, hold on. The Congressmonst—I mean, Barney—for you on line 2.

All right now—*chuckle*—enough of that.

In the end, it turned out to be both a nationalized campaign, with voters registering unhappiness with Reagan's budget cuts, and a local one, where Barney simply ran the better race.

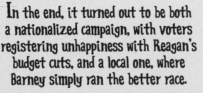

LaRouchie
Mad at REAGAN
LIKES BARNEY
DisLikes PEGGY

VOTE HERE

Exultant at the election night party in Fall River—city of his political salvation—he grabbed the mic when returns gave him 62% of the vote!

FRANK

A funny thing happened on our way to defeat...

It was finally over. After three nonstop years of running for Congress, it looked like he'd earned himself a safe seat...

We won!

But it had taken its toll. Riding home after the party, he switched on NPR just in time to hear Cokie Roberts say:

I'll tell you what happened in that race. Margaret got crazier and Barney got fatter.

He'd reached 270 pounds by election night.

Thanks, sis, couldn't have done it without you.

You're right. Get some sleep. And take a few days. Go to Florida...

He rented a family friend's condo and mostly slept and read detective novels.

By Day Three he had emptied the fridge, and he went off in search of provisions.

PUBLIX

OJ, Sanka, a bag of store-brand sandwich cookies. He put a coffee cake back, reluctantly. With Election Day over, he had no excuse not to try to lose weight.

Sigh.

A nice-looking guy in a Yale golf shirt might have stared at him invitingly. A tingle in his dick (and then everywhere else)...

...that had been entirely absent for months and months was suddenly back.

But a week after getting reelected to high federal office while denying rumors about his personal life probably wasn't the time to embark on sexual exploration by cruising grocery store aisles.

Maybe there'd never be a good time, he thought. He was over forty, mostly still in the closet. Overweight. Not a catch. Yale Golf walked on.

The sad thoughts didn't last long. He'd held on to his important job protecting those who needed his help: old people, gay people, working people—who lacked the skills he had.

Those skills—the democratic equivalent of sword & armor—had proved potent in the vote against Heckler. He'd emerged stronger politically than he'd ever been before. The thought occurred to him: What was he waiting for?

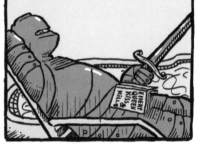

He cut the vacation short and flew back to DC the next day...

...and began his second term by taking better care of himself...

...and breaking the habits of a lifetime.

We're delighted to welcome tonight's speaker. **A shockingly svelte** Congressman Barney Frank of Massachusetts. **YAY!**

Woohoo!

But even the new-and-improved Barney remained pretty lonely at home.

Which is where he sat on a Sunday at the end of March— his forty-fifth birthday.

Outside, Washington was its typical springtime miasma of damp, cold, and drizzle.

He fished around his gym bag for the free gay rag he'd grabbed after working out earlier...

...and flipped through it. He'd been consuming great journalism since he was a kid. So why was he bothering with the *Blade* when he could be reading the *Washington Post*?

Because they don't print stories about Kaposi sarcoma... or why it's "impolite" to talk about AIDS at Georgetown parties.

Because sometimes he needed to remind himself who he really was.

He flipped the paper over and scrutinized the classifieds. Most held no interest...

Young Masseur
please call (202) Hap-yend

Tall Athletic Bavarian
Avail for Beer Garden Lederhosen fun

NO.

Not my thing.

Feelin' Frisky
75 but look 90 haha ha gotta hava sense of humor boys

Sounds screwy, like someone's weird uncle on a swingles cruise.

GWM Professor
45, 6" 150 lbs attractive Healthy stable, loving intelligent looking for similar for good times and possible relationship

No. Will immediately reject me for not being out at work.

But another caught his eye...

Exceptionally good looking
Personable
Muscular athlete is available
Hot Bottom + Large
Endowment = Good Times
(202) HOT-SEXY

He picked up the phone, a tool wielded commandingly at work but held doubtfully now, and punched in the phone number.

An engaging, regular-guy-sounding voice answered. Said he was booked for today but could do tomorrow.

Monday. A different world from his lonely Sundays. He booked anyway.

A day later, Barney opened the door to his garden (otherwise known as his basement) flat, and met a guy calling himself Steve.

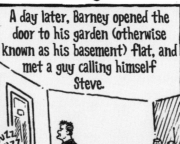

He liked the guy's looks.

Steve strode inside, made a crack about the décor, and shed his clothes.

Nice place. (Kinda.)

The guy's confidence was a turn-on. So was his appearance.

You work on the Hill?

Why do you ask?

Stack of *Federal Registers* by the couch.

His nice physique compensated for the fact that the sex was a little perfunctory. Like a pilot with a checklist.

Not so much into kissing. Shall we get down to it?

He gave the guy $85 for services rendered, thanked him for stopping by, and closed the door, satisfied.

He saw Steve again...

I'm straight, actually. Doin' it with guys is really just a money thing. To pay for school. Or maybe my own business.

Oh, huh. OK.

...and again and again.

Steve claimed to live in a house in Dupont Circle with his girlfriend.

This suited Barney fine. He was definitely not ready to explain a boyfriend to the papers back in his district.

EXTRA! EXTRA!
READ ALL ABOUT IT!
The Herald News
BARNEY'S BOYFRIEND BOMBSHELL!

17.
HUSTLE

Soon Steve was hanging around the office, paid out of Barney's pocket to run errands...

Oh good—you're here. Can you run down to pick up my shirts?

Yeah, OK.

GRUMBLE

Hiding the Daily Racing Form

Here's $20. Remember the receipt.

Want me to pick up lunch?

I ate. But OK.

Get yourself lunch. Here's $25.

Staff didn't like this arrangement.

Barney let him use his shitbox car and gave him a spare set of keys so he could do odd jobs around the apartment.

There was something pleasing about having this nice young guy as part of his household...

Hey, beautiful, just hangin' at Sweet 'n' Low's* place.

* His dumb nickname for Barney— meaning "nice and not rich."

Like having a handsome, if slightly bummy, nephew around to let the gas guy in to read the meter, or change the burned-out bulb in the bathroom.

C'mon over and light up with me.

And if the kid got the occasional parking ticket, well, it was hardly a *federal case.* DC mostly waived citations if you had congressional plates anyway.

Maybe he was taking advantage, freeloading a bit, but isn't that what good-looking young guys did?

PICKLES

FISH OIL (FROM MOM)

COFFEE CAKE

WHITE WINE (NO CORK)

MILK (EXPIRED)

Sara Lee

BROWN BANANA

WEEK-OLD RESTAURANT LEFTOVERS

He'd been convicted for coke possession at some point. Barney wrote a probation officer saying Steve was straightening out...

By this point his friend Joe had joined Barney's staff as an assistant, answering mail, tracking issues.

Joe, can you mail this?

Sure, Barn'.

His status as a friend as well as employee meant he was quick to have an opinion.

I'm tellin' ya, this "Steve" is an f'ing grifter.

I hear you, but what can I possibly do about it?

Barney didn't pay much attention, and things went on like this for a year, and then for nearly another...

Ahem. About Steve.

Steve who?

Steve, your personal assistant.

Doug, you're my chief of staff at the office, not at **home.**

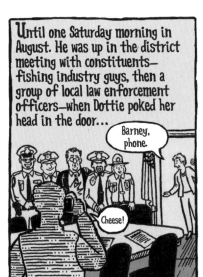
Until one Saturday morning in August. He was up in the district meeting with constituents—fishing industry guys, then a group of local law enforcement officers—when Dottie poked her head in the door...

Barney, phone.

Cheese!

His landlady was on the line.

Young people. Loud music. Partying. Reefer. Maybe more. They look like... um, hustlers. Street kids.

Gentlemen, coffee and donuts?

You're telling me there are people who look like, what? Prostitutes? **In my apartment?**

Well, I couldn't say for certain, Barney, of course!

But that's what you're suggesting? Please, PLEASE get to the point, I have a meeting.

Well, I'm sorry if you don't have the time, Congressman. **But I need to know what is going on in my house.** And yes, frankly, they look like *hookers*. And some young men who look like, well, *young male hookers!*

And other men come through the gate at all hours! **Something** is going on down there whenever you're away, and it's got to stop!

He hung up and dialed Steve's pager. After ten minutes he tried again. And again a few minutes later.

On the fourth try, Steve rang back, sounding groggy (or something)...

Christ, Sweet 'n' Low, I thought you were in Mass. Why're you callin' so freakin' early?

What the fuck, Steve!

Sorry to cut things short. Always something going on in DC, heh heh.

I just got a call from my landlady saying people are streaming in and out of my apartment!

135

Hey, relax, Sweet 'n' Low. It's just several of my besties. Y'know, to hang out and chill once in a while. Really, no biggie.

SEVERAL? ONCE IN A WHILE? I gave you my key so you could do odd jobs over there, not throw parties.

Knew that dude was trouble.

Hey, y'know what would be cool? Take an early flight back here and you can hang with us. That'll put you in a better mood.

After two years, his fugue state when it came to Steve broke hard.

Y'know, Steve, I THINK WE BETTER CALL IT QUITS.

You knew about this?

No Ma'am.

He was alarmed. God knows what this kid might be up to. How stupid had he been to trust him?

YOU'VE GOT FIFTEEN MINUTES TO GET OUT. AND, UH, DON'T CALL ME!

Wait, what the fuck, Swee—

SERIOUSLY, I WANT YOU OUT, NOW!

The locksmith came that afternoon. Relieved that the situation seemed to be under control, Barney admitted to himself that he'd grown pretty bored of the kid's company...

MAN OF THE YEAR MASS. FAIR HOUSING COALITION

ELEANOR & ADLAI

Everything OK, boss?

Did I say anything about *not being* OK? Please. This is not a shrink's office. Send in my next appointment.

The side of himself that wasn't born yesterday— the side involving every aspect of his life other than being gay—finally reasserted itself.

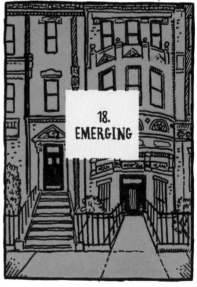

18.
EMERGING

His coming-out had been interrupted by his initial bid for Congress, and then by his nasty race against Mrs. Heckler a few years later...

It had been easier just not to think about it—and to deny it if asked—and if you weren't thinking or doing anything, well, really, *what was there to say*, he bargained with himself.

Now though, by 1987, something about the break with Steve caused a leap in his thinking.

It's me.

For his own peace of mind— really, for his own sanity— it was time to be open about his sexuality.

Hi, Ma. Was in Cambridge. Bought you some bialys.

He told Elsie. She was unfazed.

MMMWAA. Thank you. Give me a sec to get my bag.

You should take those bialys. You're too thin. Hey, this Iran-Contra stuff is crazy!

SO WHAT? It's not like I'm sitting around waiting on an eighth grandchild. It's not like you aren't the same wonderful kid who left school to help out when your father died. If anyone wants to make an issue of it, send them to me.

Thanks, Ma.

He went to see Kevin, who was surprised, then changed the subject.

Oh. Uh. That so? Well.

He wondered if queenier guys had an easier time coming out.

Hey, you ever been to Barcelona? No?

Marvelous town.

Still, he was glad he'd done it.

Want a lift?

Nah. Green Line's a straight shot to Newton.

Not that straight, apparently.

Having cut off his unhealthy relationship with Steve, he knew it was time to start being honest with himself,

with the people around him, and with the people who elected him. But he hesitated. Until someone gave him a little push...

Bob Bauman was a stridently right-wing congressman from Maryland, implacably against abortion and gay rights, despite the twisted fact that Bauman was gay himself.

A few years back, he'd lost his seat after a scandal with an underaged rent boy.

The Demonic Firewater, yea, alcohol, is to blame for my travails.

And my big cock!

Right around the time that Barney broke it off with Steve, now ex-congressman Bob Bauman wrote a book about his being forced from office. He bitterly denounced what he saw as a double standard...

THE DEVIL MADE ME DO It*

* Truth be told, the book's title was GENTLEMAN FROM MARYLAND

...where conservative gay members of Congress were outed by the media, while liberal members—and here Bauman specifically named Barney—weren't.

But the bone that the media was chewing on wasn't really a member's sexuality, it was his **hypocrisy**—especially if he fought against LGBT rights back home while sneakily enjoying the benefits of vibrant gay city life in DC.

In 1980–81 Bauman supported the noxious McDonald Amendment to deny legal services assistance to gays.

Anyway, Barney hustled over to Kramers in Dupont Circle as soon as Bauman's nasty book hit store shelves.

He Washing-skimmed (checked the index for the page numbers with his name).

But instead of feeling alarm—or horror as he flipped to the pages that outed him publicly for the first time—he felt weirdly calm.

You want me to ring it up, Congressman?

WHAT? Uh...no. Thanks.

It was a long subway ride. He'd passed Shame, Self-Loathing, Furtiveness, Fear, Waiting-for-Just-the-Right-Moment, and finally, here he was, pulling into Enough's Enough.

He rushed to Speaker O'Neill's office.

He's on the floor, Congressman. Something came up about Nicaragua.

HUFF HUFF

So he ran upstairs and into the chamber...

...then down the center aisle and up the steps to the rostrum.

Mr. Speaker, a moment of your time in the cloakroom?

Of course, Representative.

Cardiss, do you mind stepping up here to take the helm for a bit?

My pleasure, Speaker.

Matthews, help Congresswoman Collins up to the podium.

Yessir, on it.

What's going on, pal?

Tip, Bob Bauman wrote a book. Hit the stores today. He outs me as being gay.

Aw, Bahney, is that all?

Don't pay no mind, my boy. We're pols! People're always spreading shit about us!

Problem is, in this case, Mr. Speaker, it's true. And I think its time to say so publicly.

OH! Well damn, Bahney. I'm sorry to hear that. Was hoping you'd wind up being the first Jewish Speaker. Now I guess I'll haft'a hope you'll be the first gay, Jewish Speaker.

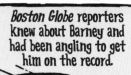

Boston Globe reporters knew about Barney and had been angling to get him on the record.

Well well, if it isn't the Boring Broadsheet's best cowgirl.

In the flesh, mama. Is he ready?

Take a seat.

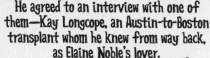

He agreed to an interview with one of them—Kay Longcope, an Austin-to-Boston transplant whom he knew from way back, as Elaine Noble's lover.

Hates whistling

1974
At a Back Bay, Boston, house party / fundraiser

Am I your first Texbian, honey?

Although Barney had first been elected in 1972, he'd been closeted. It was Elaine, in 1974, who was the first openly gay elected state official in the USA.

Lesbian from Texas? Yeah, actually.

Well, shove over, newbie, an' make some room for mah Trailblazer.

Fifteen years later, here was Kay staring intently at him across his messy desk. She flipped open a notebook and got right to the point.

So, Congressman, what's the deal? Are you gay?

After all those years, after dating girls he wouldn't love, after baldly denying it to political allies, after lying about it under oath...

After playing spin the bottle in stuffy Bayonne rumpus rooms, praying for the lights to be turned back on...

Well, that's enough of that, ladies & gentlemen. Time for everyone to go on home.

After a fucking lifetime of all that, he found himself saying:

Yeah, I am. So what?

I think the average voter says get the bridges built. Stop nukes. Find shelter for the homeless, and don't steal from the till. I'm hoping they don't give a damn about who I care to love or have sex with.

Good for you, darlin'.

Remember to breathe!

Still, back then, it was big news when a public figure came out...

To Barney's relief, the reaction was positive.

Hey, whaddevah floats yor boat.

I should fix him up with my son.

It turned out that for most voters, his being gay didn't matter any more than his failure to ever shine his shoes...

...or to love kissing babies. Their bottom line seemed to be *"He fights on issues that matter."* And on the bullshitty side of politics, they were happy to cut him some slack and reelect him overwhelmingly.

And another nice thing came of coming out...

A lot are from nice ladies in Brookline. But also from gay kids in Detroit and Orange County. And lesbians from upstate NY and queer men from just about everywhere else.

TEARING UP

...hundreds of supportive letters from all across the country.

Among the letters was one from a thirty-year-old guy named Herb.

You want the LCs* to start drafting responses?

No, I'll write them myself.

DEFINITELY NOT TEARING UP

FOOMP

* legislative correspondents (junior staffers)

Herb sounded nice. Barney closed his office door and called to ask him out for coffee.

Thanks for your very kind note.

And he did turn out to be nice. And nice looking, in a mensch-y sort of way...

Also kindly, low-key, and interested in politics. He was completing a graduate degree in economics.

I'll have what she's having...

They went on a proper date, and then on another.

They had plain old romantic sex like he knew from the movies.

Herb seemed mature and thougtful. Soon they were spending their weekends together.

He didn't bring up his tortured sexual past of recent years. And Herb didn't ask.

After graduating, Herb looked for a job as an economist with one of the federal agencies. Barney wrote to the CEO of Fannie Mae, the giant mortgage company. Herb landed a job as an analyst.

And just like that, he'd transformed into a guy who, for the first time in his life, had an entirely conventional social life.

But if it was conventional by gay romance standards, it trailblazed politically.

How should the first-ever same-sex-coupled member of Congress behave?

He looked to the example of Adam Clayton Powell, the great clergyman from Harlem who in 1944 became the only Black member of Congress—

and he emulated Powell's dignified but steely insistence on full rights in a House of Representatives controlled by Southern racists.

Powell had demanded use of every bathroom, dining room, gym—every single privilege he had coming as a duly elected member of Congress.

Barney did the same. And life was better for a few years than he'd ever dared hope it could be.

He took Herb to the White House Christmas party.

Mr. President, Madame First Lady, this is my boyfriend.

Hey there!

The stability and satisfaction he'd found personally seemed to boost his effectiveness professionally.

That was AMAZING!

He became more and more knowledgeable about housing finance...

We should subpoena Watt.

...pushing for more affordable rental apartments and housing for the elderly across the county.

Schedule a hearing.

NATIONAL HOUSING ACT OF 1934

CHILI

At the same time, the Republicans were demonizing fictional welfare queens as the embodiment of wasteful government spending run amok.

He was intent on providing a counterpoint to that racist narrative, by showcasing the corruption occuring within the Republican-led HUD.

We got them dead to rights. Look.

Good.

His staff had identified millions of scarce HUD money being funneled to Republican donors to do bogus consulting work for real estate developers.

More pizza & coffee?

Yep.

And he opened a congressional probe.

So Mr. Watt, you have absolutely no experience in the affordable housing field, and yet you were paid $300,000 by developers to lobby HUD on their behalf. Why would they pay you all that cash for something you know nothing about?

I didn't do nothing, Mr. Frank, I picked up the phone to call the proper authorities to help! I called my friend, the Secretary of Housing and Urban Development.

Wait, a phone call from you is worth three hundred grand?

I made THREE OF THEM!

Huh. Remind me never to get a flat in front of your house. My phone bill's expensive enough without you calling a tow truck and demanding a hundred grand for doing so.

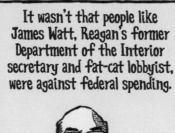

It wasn't that people like James Watt, Reagan's former Department of the Interior secretary and fat-cat lobbyist, were against federal spending.

It was that they were against federal spending for poor people.

When Congress suspended for its August break, all of DC anticipated that Barney would be back in the fall with a new slate of hearings designed to spotlight corporate welfare and corruption.

Nice job, Congressman.

See ya next month, Darryl.

DC is wonderfully still during the summer recess. Its humidity isn't really that oppressive if you aren't encased in a suit or yoked to a tie. Even staffers who remain on duty relish the slower workdays...

Sigh.

...the sane pace, the chance to catch up on research, kicking off early for a run (or a nap) down in the weirdly cooler climes of Rock Creek Park.

For the first few days off, he enjoyed walking to a nearby diner each morning for coffee and the newspapers.

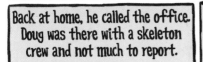

But he was looking forward to Saturday, when he and Herb were headed to Provincetown for a couple of weeks…

For the first time since he was a kid, he couldn't wait to go on vacation.

You taking any time off, brother?

Yes, Congressman. Cape Cod.

Nice.

REP. JOHN LEWIS

Back at home, he called the office. Doug was there with a skeleton crew and not much to report.

A few press calls about your HUD hearing, and some invites for September that Dottie's handling.

OK, Michael J. Fox is sooo cute.

Sorry, that was Marcia.

He hung up. A lawn mower's drone through an open window was making him drowsy. He was thinking of taking a nap—

when the sound of the doorbell startled him.

BUZZ BUZZ

He glanced out the front window (doable, now that Herb had replaced the Hefty bags).

CONGRESSMAN FRANK! HEYAH!

Yeah?

We're from the Washington Times.

Can we ask you a few questions?

He rolled his eyes. So weird that Reverend Moon now owned a paper in DC. He wondered if these were actual Moonies. He'd never met one.

Yeah. Reporters usually call though.

What about?

Steven Gobie.

Do you know him, Congressman?

He tried to mask his distress at hearing that name.

Not anymore.

HA! But you did!

Yeah. That's what "not anymore" implies, Sherlock.

Hot out here. You guys want coffee? Water?

Yeah, we'll take water. So about Gobie—

He's told us that between 1985 and 1987, he was employed as a male escort.

And that during these years you repeatedly paid him for sex.

He'd seen enough politicians ruin their careers by lying about sex. So he didn't.

Yup.

GASP

Wait, you admit it?

PULITZER PRIZE

Yeah. Not lately. I was closeted. I assume you two geniuses know the term? I was very unhappy as a result.

So yeah, for a time I paid that person for sex.

147

And after that ended?
He did odd jobs for me until about two years ago, after which he didn't.
And during the two years that he worked for you, did you offer him any help with his business?
CLICK
What business?
His escort business. C'mon, Congressman, his *pimping.*
Of course not. Wait—his **pimping?**
Yes. Here. In your apartment.
HIS PIMPING IN MY APARTMENT?
WHAT ARE YOU GOONS TALKING ABOUT?
Mr. Gobie has given the *Washington Times* a sworn statement claiming that between 1985 and 1987, he ran a brothel from this location with your full knowledge and consent. We're just here for your side of a credible story before we publish this
Steaming pile of bullshit!

I was going to say **blockbuster investigative expose.**

So, any further comment?

Look, I admitted what is true. The rest is completely fucked.

So that's a denial?

Yeah, that's a denial.

Hey, how about that water, Congressman? Sex scandal's a thirsty business.

SLAM!

19.
SHIT

Shit shit shit shit SHIT. He picked up the phone to call the office. Put it down again, trying not to feel panicky and failing...

...called again and barked at an intern to put Doug on the line.

The Moonie paper's gonna print an expose.

It's gonna be bad.

Um, he doesn't want us to stay past 3 PM, does he? Because our internship advisor expressly said—

ABOUT WHAT?

JEEZ. Excuse YOU!

MY SEX LIFE!

Fuck.

What's going on?

Got any painkillers?

A few Advil.

Was hoping morphine, but OK.

He called Jimmy, spilled his guts about the whole mess.

Slow down, Barn'. Let's not panic. Maybe they won't even publish it.

Same with his big sister, Ann.

Should he get a lawyer?

No. We need to wait for the story to drop. Just hold on.

Guess I'll cancel our court time.

He'd have to tell Herb. Oh shit. HE'D HAVE TO TELL HERB.

These white Levi's will look great on me in PTown.

He had feverish conference calls with Segel and others.

We need to know what's being alleged. And by whom.

Just the Moonie rag? Or is there a prosecutor poking around?

If this is just about a hooker, they'd have to arrest the whole goddamn town.

Except for Tip.

Question is: Do we need a criminal lawyer? Or just a good PR agent?

It was all so absurd. The fucking Everleigh Sisters his basement one-bedroom definitely wasn't. Who in their right mind would mistake his place for a bordello?

ADA EVERLEIGH NOTORIOUS GILDED AGE MADAM

Wasn't it solicitation that's illegal? He'd *ANSWERED* Steve's ad in that newspaper. How was answering soliciting?

It was an excruciating forty-eight hours. If he slept at all, it was brief.

Then it was over. Doug, his DC chief of staff, called. It was on the *Washington Times*'s front page.

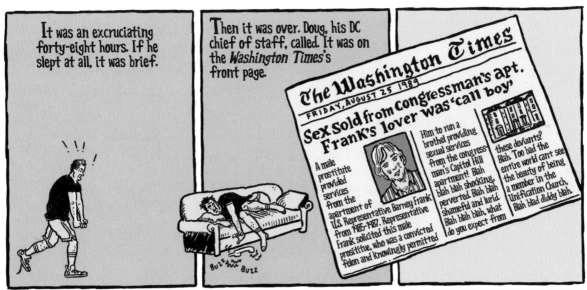

The Washington Times
FRIDAY, AUGUST 25 1989
Sex sold from congressman's apt. Frank's lover was 'call boy'

A male prostitute provided services from the apartment of U.S. Representative Barney Frank from 1985-1987. Representative Frank solicited this male prostitute, who was a convicted felon and knowingly permitted

Him to run a brothel providing sexual services from the congressman's Capitol Hill apartment! Blah blah blah shocking, perverted! Blah blah shameful and lurid. Blah blah blah, what do you expect from

these deviants? Blah. Too bad the entire world can't see the beauty of being a member in the Unification Church. Blah blad diddly blah

---

Buried in its story, the Moonie paper covered its ass by stating that Steve had flunked a polygraph...

No, man, for reals, this's how it all went down.

...then breezily dismissed the lie detector's results by stating falsely that Barney had confirmed most of the allegations.

ashington Time

Oh yes! Mr. Frank practically admitted to all of it.

Herb was shell-shocked at first, but then rallied...

Whatever you need me to do, I'll do, Barney.

LONELY PLANET PTOWN

Barney called Elsie to tell her to steel herself. Which wasn't a problem.

They don't call it helmet hair for nothin'

AQUA Net

What?

Never mind. I love you.

Doug, Jimmy, Dottie, and Ann (flabbergasted but a political pro in her own right—too busy fighting the fire to worry about how it started) all agreed he needed to hold a press conference.

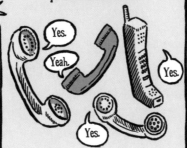

Yes.

Yeah.

Yes.

Yes.

Boss, we need to do this back in the district, as far away from K Street call boys as we can get.

4TH CONGRESSIONAL DISTRICT

How about the Newton Community Center gym?

Agreed.

Congressman, do you regularly seek out gigolos for sex?

Congressman, tell us a little about your circular waterbed.

And the sex dungeon stuff. Whaddya got by way of that? Harnesses? Whips? Slings? How about slings?

Congressman, when the customers couldn't get in touch with Steve, did they call your Capitol Hill office to, say, book an appointment, or request a different call girl or boy?

Congressman, the sex workers themselves, do you socialize with them off the clock as well as on?

He answered question after humiliating question from a big contingent of local and national reporters, all crammed into a Newton gym. It was a real effing zoo.

Congressman, what was your cut for each trick?

Again, he admitted to having hired Steve for sex...

Yeah, I did. Look, as a closeted man in a high-profile world, I didn't know how to meet somebody.

....and acknowledged invoking his congressional privilege to waive Gobie's parking tickets.

I'm embarrassed to admit that I saw myself as a sort of Henry Higgins.

I thought he was a guy who wanted help.

But he adamantly denied knowing about Steve's prostitution ring.

The idea that I knew about that is just crazy.

CONGRESSMAN, YOU GONNA QUIT?

Look, it would be pretty arrogant to go forward as if nothing happened. I don't own this job. I know I've got to earn it.

If I've become a liability when it comes to pushing the issues I care about, well, I'll know it's time to do something else.

Finally they ran out of questions and the presser broke up. The TV people were friendly off camera.

Hang tough, Barn'.

Even the hard-bitten print reporters were moved. It wasn't often that such a high-ranking pol cops to such a mess.

You poor sonuvabitch.

21. Survival Tactics

They walked the several blocks back to his district office—a nondescript suite in a suburban office building filled with orthodontists and accountants.

The AC blasted and the phones rang off the hook. Dottie had a surprising tally on her desk. Calls were running four to one in support of Barney...

Erv, why not order everyone some lunch.

Will do.

They picked up some sandwiches, but no one really felt like eating. Actually, they all felt a little sick to their stomachs.
OK, we need a strategy.
Barney, eat.
Not hungry, Ma.
Back in DC, Herb watched the press conference on TV and realized how serious the situation was.
Shit.
Saving Barney's career was going to be all-consuming for the foreseeable future...
All of it's embarrassing, but none of it's criminal.
So what do we do?
We call for a full investigation.
Yeah. Get out in front.
Maybe.
I think you're right. Only way I'm gonna clear my name is if the Ethics Committee proves *he's* lying.
I'll draft the request.
He was so sad—knew he'd let them all down terribly. Told them to cancel an appearance at a parade in Fall River on his schedule for the next day...
Fat chance.
His mom, his siblings, and Herb all joined him. They walked the entire parade route together. To his surprise, the crowd cheered supportively.
It's OK, Bahney!
Weez still with ya!
So cheer the fuck up!

But the scandal didn't abate. The *Washington Times* followed up with new, more outrageous allegations.

AUGUST 30, 1989
Call Boy Tells All
WASHINGTON D.C.—

BACK TO SCHOOL

VOYAGER 2 NEARS NEPTUNE

The claims weren't corroborated, but it didn't seem to matter. Other media outlets picked up the story and ran with it.

If I wanted to ruin half of DC, all I'd have to do is open my Rolodex.

All this was too much for the middle-aged, mostly Irish guys at the *Globe*. Macho liberals, like their heroes Jack and Bobby—but still a bit prudish about anything sexual.

The next Sunday they penned a damning lead editorial from their newsroom-cum–Mount Olympus on Morrissey Boulevard.

Boston Sunday Globe

At issue is not homosexuality, but prostitution, which is illegal, and the reason why, in this family newspaper's opinion, BARNEY FRANK MUST GO.

The Boston Globe

The editorial hurt. He'd known those *Globe* guys for years. And it added to the scandal's momentum.

Who cares what a few ex-altar boys at the *Boston Globe* think?

Me. And everyone else I know, except, thankfully, you.

Rep. William Dannemeyer, Capitol Hill's version of a Grimms' fairy-tale troll living under a bridge, spewed ignoramus-ness from the House floor.

Now listen to this, my colleagues, because this next part is about "rimming." Did Frank practice this? Let's find out!

MOVE

ALARMED 6TH GRADE FIELD TRIP

"JOY OF GAY SEX"

TV talking head and sometimes-Nazi apologist Pat Buchanan got off a few good lines.

Frank has no place attacking mismanagement at HUD when he couldn't spot a whorehouse in his own basement.

RADIO WOLFSSCHANZE

SS

Johnny Carson piled on at night.

Representative Barney Frank claims he didn't know what his assistant was doing. Barney, when your aide shows up for work in a Chippendales bow tie and underwear, that's a clue.

Newsweek ran a cover story.

A scandal that so plainly reflects discredit on the House of Representatives and on the gay rights movement that some of Mr. Frank's former allies are quickly deserting him.

Newsweek
BARNEY FRANK'S DOUBLE LIFE

But the allies who really counted, the voters of his district, did not seem to be deserting him at all.

Ring!

Who could that be?

Whoever it is, tell 'em don't call during *St. Elsewhere.*

Polls showed his constituents were sticking with him.

We still like Bahney, he does a good job.

Even if he was running against a happily married (to a woman) man with three kids?

Nah. we'd stick with the Bahnster.

Hmm. What if he was running against a movie star? Or a famous football coach? What if he was running against Doug Flutie?

The good poll numbers were a relief—one that provided the breathing room needed for his sister Doris and others to let him have it.

Do you have any idea how much family and career time I sacrificed so you could get this job? How could you be so cavalier?

He moped around feeling sorry for himself until Elsie, who was coming to the office every day to help out, had had enough.

Get back to work! You aren't quitting

just because putzes at the *Globe* say so.

As an employee, albeit one with solid political standing of her own, Dottie wasn't about to bawl out her boss.

RAVEL
WE
WTON
CI MA

She had loved her back-to-back life running the in-state political operations for two high-profile and dynamic members of Congress...

But here she was about to turn 60, racing through Newton at the crack of dawn to make it to the office for her 7:30 crisis communications conference call for maybe the eleventh day in a row.

It was exhausting to find herself for the second time in a decade consumed with the end of her boss's career.

Even so, she felt protective of him, the way you might when a normally good teenager fucks up royally.

After the initial shock, his defenders found their voices...

Won't this piss off upstairs?

Fuck upstairs.

CLACK

Tom Oliphant, a *Globe* correspondent, penned a pro-Barney column.

In Fall River, the mayor went on TV and said:

Sticking with Barney is in our own best interests.

And the LGBT community especially seemed to understand how a person could be smart in one arena of life and pretty dumb in another.

We been there, baby.

By October, anger at getting kicked around by the right wing began to overtake shame and embarrassment.

He went back to DC and tried to remind himself that his life wasn't the sordid mess the *Globe* claimed it was. Not anymore, anyway.

I'm taking you out for dinner.

In December, the House Ethics Committee finally started to investigate the allegations against Barney.

Gobie testified. Sitting at a green-felt-covered table in an out-of-the-way hearing room at the Capitol, he undercut his preppy assistant-professor look with darting drug dealer eyes.

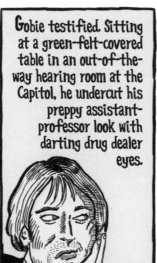

Sweet 'n' Low—sorry—I mean, Mr. Frank—was in DC on the dates I have stated, and was fully aware of sex occurring for payment in his residence on those days.

But these phone and travel records show Rep. Frank in Massachusetts on the dates you allege.

Oh, *also,* Barney and I had hot and steamy sex in the House gym.

But the House gym has considerable security, and there's no evidence you've ever set foot in it.

Then it was Barney's turn to testify.

My judgment was very faulty.

I was very lonely.

His landlady sent a sworn affidavit to the committee.

It is my firm belief that Mr. Gobie misused the apartment without Congressman Frank's knowledge or permission.

In the end, all but two minor charges were dismissed.

Congressman Frank wasn't candid when writing to Mr. Gobie's probation officer about how they met. Congressman Frank should not have written *"through mutual friends."*

Second, Congressman Frank shouldn't have used congressional privilege to seek the waiver of nine parking tickets incurred by Gobie while driving Frank's car.

Lunch? You bet.

Later, those Ethics Committee members who were more sympathetic to Barney pushed for relatively light punishment—a letter of reproval. Others demanded expulsion.

No fuckin' way!

He says "no fuckin' way."

Flip?

YOU BETTER BELIEVE **WAY**.

Well, that's a deadlock. Hey, it's Thursday. Let's go fundraise.

Eventually they settled on a **reprimand**—more than a wrist slap, less than expulsion. Their recommendation was sent to the House floor for a vote.

Reprimand

PAGES

Congressman Dannemeyer and his obnoxious Orange County twin, Congressman Bob Dornan, were furious.

He has besmirched our Judeo-Christian foundation...

...and the standards God gave to man!

Expel him!

He sat contritely on the Dem side. Members came over to squeeze his shoulder and offer support while the Neanderthals thundered on. Eventually, the House voted overwhelmingly to reject their calls for expulsion.

Among the few who DID vote to expel was Denny Hastert, future Speaker, felon, and pervy wrestling coach.

Newt Gingrich—soon to have an affair with a staffer that would break the heart of his dying second wife—demanded Barney's censure. The House voted that one down too.

Larry Craig—who would become famous for his WIDE STANCE technique for cruising dudes in airport restrooms—voted with Newt.

159

I am here to apologize to my colleagues, and to offer an explanation.

For most of my life, there was a central element of dishonesty. It had to do with my privacy and my private life. To conceal my sexual orientation, I misrepresented my relationship with this man.
I should've known better. I do now. But it's a little late.
Finally, it was his turn to address the House.

When it was over, the vote was 408 to 18 in favor of the Ethics Committee's middle-of-the-road compromise—reprimand.

Eleven right wingers and seven liberals opposed reprimand, for different reasons, obviously.

Nancy Pelosi was a newly elected member. She voted against reprimand because she thought it was too harsh a punishment and also because, pardon her French—

It's BULLSHIT.

As soon as the vote was over, he left the House chamber.

Ignoring the members' subway, he walked through the fluorescent-lit tunnels under the Capitol.

He needed to move. To feel his arms and legs and body after what had been, for months, an out-of-body experience.

Ten minutes later he reached the Rayburn Building...

We're with ya, Congressman.

He climbed three flights of oversized marble stairs, then walked down the long corridor to his office.

His staff was waiting for him, some smiling, some tearing up. He mumbled thank-yous, then retreated behind his office door.

SLAM

NOK

That fall, his Republican opponent for Congress excitedly tried to use the scandal against him…

I've passed an "AIDS test," Congressman. Have you?

That may be the *only* test you've ever passed.

When will you release the results of your AIDS test, Congressman?

I'll tell you what: I promise to release the results of my HIV test if you promise to release the results of your IQ test.

…to no avail. In November, Barney was reelected overwhelmingly.

Re-elect BARNEY

A few days later the *Boston Globe* sheepishly published a new editorial.

"We thought the revelation of squalor in his private life would hamper his effectiveness beyond repair. We were wrong, and we now foresee a long and fruitful career for Barney Frank."

His ordeal was finally over.

22.
GAY
'90s.

So the voters sent him back to Capitol Hill. The question remained, though: How would the Hill receive him?

Rayburn Building.

WASHINGTON NATIONAL AIRPORT

OK, Congressman.

Some members come back to serve yet another term in Congress after having been caught stashing payola in their freezers.

Or after having become nearly inanimate with old age.

Or after having run for president on a platform stressing belief in UFOs.

Holy cow, Shirley, wait'll the American people hear about this!

Sure, they still held office. But whether colleagues or staff still respected them was an entirely different issue.

Mornin', Congressman Kucinich. How's them aliens?

You won't laugh when they land and colonize.

He wondered if they'd still joke with him in the cloakroom.

Would they still ask him how to vote on a bill they hadn't read, but knew he had?

Hey, Barn', that the crime bill? Motherfucker's like 900 pages, huh?

Would they still want his help pushing their projects through committee because he knew the arcane rules better than the parliamentarians themselves?

So, wait, motion to recommit?

No. Motion to reconsider.

The fact that he'd survived legally and politically didn't magically take these insecurities away.

Hey, babe, what's that?

A pot I made for you in ceramics class.

Despite Herb's doing the best he could to distract him.

I don't have a pot. Thank you.

Well, now you do. Got time to join me in the bedroom before your event tonight?

Would love to.

In 1991, President George H. W. Bush seemed likely to win reelection after Operation Desert Storm had kicked Saddam Hussein out of Kuwait.

Poppy seemed poised to bring along a slew of new Republican members of Congress on his coattails...

In this atmosphere of needing all the help they could get, the Democratic leadership found Barney's skills too useful for benching...

Speaker! What can I do for you, sir?

Assignment fer you, compadre.

FEDERAL HOUSING ACT OF 1947

Tip O'Neill had retired. Texan Jim Wright was Speaker.

He was put on the Budget Committee, which has a say in how every taxpayer dollar is spent.

SPORTS

Which meant he was at the center of things when then Secretary of Defense (and future vice president) Dick Cheney testified before the committee.

Other members at the hearing asked Cheney about:

The goddamn Sovietskis...

Are they collapsin' or what?

What about Saddam? Should we chase that mother-fucker all the way back to Baghdad or what?

Eventually, it was Barney's turn.

It's been forty years since President Eisenhower signed an executive order...

...deeming all gay and lesbian persons working for the federal government, including the military, to be an inherent security risk because they are subject to blackmail by foreign agents. Is that still the government's policy?

But here's the thing: Cheney's right-hand man, Assistant Sec. of Defense Pete Williams, was a closeted gay man. Barney knew this, and he'd quietly made sure that Cheney knew that he knew.

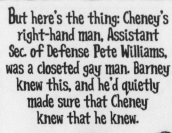

So Cheney understood that if he defended the exclusion of gays from federal service, he risked Barney asking why Cheney's own Pentagon deputy was gay.

So Cheney was trapped. And he surprised everyone at the hearing by saying:

Well, frankly, Congressman, that policy's a bit of an old chestnut.

Translated for anyone who isn't a stuffy, middle-aged white guy swilling bourbon at a men's club, Cheney meant: in this day and age, there's nothing inherently risky about a federal agent or a member of the armed services who happens to be gay.

Barney had set Cheney up, and in giving an off-the-cuff answer, the future VP wound up weakening one of the government's most long-standing homophobic policies—

Woohoo!

the ban on gays in the military—and explicitly repudiated another, the Eisenhower executive order. It was just a dry exchange between two guys in a hearing room...

Ahem.

Sitting back down now.

...but on some days, what happens in those rooms can change America forever.

Have you no decency, sir?

Army-McCarthy Hearings, 1954

What did the president know, and when did he know it?

Watergate Hearings, 1973

Then he said, "Who put pubic hair on my Coke?"

Clarence Thomas Hearings, 1991

Maybe today had been one of those days.

23.
Defending a Sometimes Progressive, Sometimes Triangulated, Sometimes Mortifying Presidency

By 1992, a faltering economy was undermining President George Herbert Walker Bush, who had been so popular just a year before...

We're in deep doo-doo, Bar'.

Barney endorsed a young Arkansas governor, whose energy and politics impressed him, in the Democratic presidential primaries.

Which is why I hope you'll join me in backing Bill Clinton.

SSSHUCKS. Thanks, Barney! So good to join you all here in Newton.

There's an oily side to him, but hoo-boy is he ever smart and empathetic.

TSONGAS

Though an Ivy League lawyer and a Rhodes Scholar, Clinton had the common touch.

Fellahs, it's **time to eat the donuts!**

YES!!!

And it was clear from the outset that the Arkansan had no anti-gay prejudice.

LOVE shakin' booty with y'all in PTown!

In 1992, Clinton won the presidency. And Barney's early endorsement accelerated his own political rehabilitation.

Sometimes, he and the new president agreed...

Mr. President, your Family and Medical Leave Act is an idea whose time has come. I vote aye.

Sometimes they didn't.

Free trade makes for a nice story. But in reality, we can't and shouldn't compete with foreign goods produced with slave labor and no environmental controls. I vote no on NAFTA.

And sometimes Barney and President Clinton tried—not entirely successfully—to split the difference.

Yessir, I'm gay. Though I don't really know what that has to do with the price of beans. I'm also an airborne sensor specialist and a highly ranked naval aircrew instructor.

Barely a month into Clinton's presidency, the federal court ordered the armed services to stop discharging personnel on the basis of being gay.

We find that Sailor Keith Meinhold was denied equal protection under the law as guaranteed by the Constitution of the United States of America.

The ruling meant Bill Clinton had an unexpectedly big mess on his hands.

Oh Lord, why me! Betty? Stephanopoulos? Y'all get me Barney Frank on the phone, PRONTO.

The top brass threatened to ignore the court.
Their presence will undermine unit cohesion.
While homophobes in Congress worked to maintain the gay ban.
Ovah mah dead body will homosexuals be allowed in the sacred US militarah.
At a gay pub on U Street NW
Look, Dole, Nunn, and their asshole posse have attached a rider to Clinton's Family Medical Leave Act, so the president can't get his prized bill into law without also committing the gay ban to federal law. We've gotta find a compromise.
Or it will look like we caused the first defeat of the Clinton presidency.
Dammit, it's not **our fault** the federal court finally decided that egregious homophobia should no longer be official US policy.
Amen.
What about a compromise? Like when we're on duty we can't mention our sexual orientation, when we're off duty we do what we want.
OH C'MON!
You might as well say "*gayness*" isn't appropriate in a professional setting. Are you gonna say the same thing for "*straightness*"?
So a straight submarine commander can keep a photo of his wife in his quarters, but a gay submarine commander gets shitcanned for a photo of his boyfriend?
Where's the equal protection in that?
Look, that compromise may not be perfect,
PERFECT?! It absolutely **SUCKS.**
Maybe you guys are oxygen deprived from all those years of stale closet air.
Fuck you, Joe.
Hey, if the boudoir fits.

Maybe that compromise is better in the same way that having a window in your prison cell is better, but not really. Not if you're wrongly imprisoned in the first place.

Being allowed a discreetly private life off base is better than a dishonorable discharge. It just is. And again, no one says you stop fighting there!

LATER

A window still improves on what you had before. Doesn't mean you stop fighting for freedom.

Gotta use the pisser.

Mr. President, maybe a compromise? So long as service members are quiet about their private lives while on duty, they're allowed to serve. And they can lead some semblance of a satisfying private life—without harassment by military authorities—when they're off base.

The president liked the on duty/off duty idea, though he ignored Barney's warnings that unless done carefully, it would backfire.

LOVE IT, brother. You've managed to cut the baby in two. Old King Solomon'd be impressed!

Well, Mr. President, you'd have to be careful with the implementation because if the policy was misconstrued, you could have serious—

GOTTA RUN, BARNEY!

Great talkin', brother. Let's see you and Harvey over at the residence for dinner sometime soon, hear?

Wow. **That** was something, huh?

Herb?

You awake?

Night.

You OK?

Just wondering what it's like to have the president call you at midnight for advice.

Whaddya mean? It just happened. **You know** what it would be like.

170

It just happened to **you**, Barney. **Not** to me.

I thought it happened to both of us.

Yeah, well, it didn't.

Good night.

The compromise was adopted, but without the protections Barney wanted or his support. Military brass felt they had license to ferret out even highly decorated LGBT service members.

OCWB.
BAIL-BONDS
IGLE
MP

A witch hunt ensued that ruined the professional lives of 13,000 LGBT soldiers, sailors, airmen & airwomen, and marines.

The rest of Clinton's first term was rocky. Health care didn't get passed. Black Hawk Down and Rwanda wrenched the nation and then the world. And a new LGBT issue flared up in Hawaii.

The question in a case before Hawaii's supreme court was whether the state constitution allowed gay Hawaiians to marry.

The possibility of an affirmative ruling had social conservatives across the country in full freak-out mode.

GOD HATES FAGS
GOD HATES FAGS
WESTBORO

Georgetown

But wouldn't the other states have to honor the Hawaiian marriages?

Not necessarily. Each state has its own power to govern marriage...

But what about the Constitution? Isn't it a problem to exclude some people but not other people from a—

HEY CONGRESSMAN!

Hopin' to bend your ear about that tax credit program for home builders! Won't take but two shakes of a lamb's tail!

K Street guy

Please. Please STOP. We're eating here! Call Maria at my office and make an appoint—wait, what do you want? MAKE IT FAST.

SUPER! THANKS SO MUCH, CONGRESSMAN. So in Title II of the subcommittee draft, our association of community banks thinks the language is strengthened if we...

Meanwhile, Senator Bob Dole jumped on the Hawaiian issue by ramming legislation called DOMA through Congress.

Dole had an old-timey villain sort of vibe.

And he was Clinton's Republican opponent for reelection in 1996.

Defense of Marriage Act (DOMA)

Be it resolved that Marriage across the Country is between ONE MAN and ONE WOMAN.

No other state is compelled by the US Constitution to recognize same-sex marriages performed in other states.

The president called DOMA divisive and gay-baiting. But in his exasperating, split-the-difference way, he also said:

If it makes it to my desk, I'll sign it.

Conservatives in the House claimed, hysterically, that permitting gay marriage would undermine straight marriage.

The flames of hedonism are licking at the foundations of our society.

If the flames licking my foundation were Mr. Barr, I'd douse him. But I'd hate myself in the morning.

Rep. Bob Barr

Barney thought that when these dire predictions didn't come true, the case for gay marriage would be strengthened. Wedding planners would still do a brisk business.

Check the flower girl's fingers.

The *Times'* Vows page would still be full of hedge fund offspring getting hitched...

If they're sticky, go check the cake.

VOWS

And despite the setback of DOMA, gay marriage would ultimately prevail.

Are the relationships with your spouses of such fragility that the fact that I have a loving relationship with another man jeopardizes them?

**24.
MOM, BILLY,
and Another
New District**

Meanwhile,
Elsie's senior advocacy
work had only intensified...

She rallied, she spokesperson-ed,
she testified at hearing after
hearing up on Beacon Hill.

During your last campaigns,
each of you promised seniors
better housing, better health care,
better legal protections.
Time to pay up.

And in doing so, she made the
unlikeliest of new friends: state
senate president Billy Bulger—
Barney's old
nemesis.

Coffee?

If you're
buying.

They were oddly in sync.
Both were tough, hardworking,
short, and funny. He may have run
the legislature like an autocrat,
but she liked his willingness to
spend on elder services like
a liberal.

Their new friendship became
significant in 1990 when the
new census results determined
that Massachusetts had to
lose yet another seat in
Congress.

Recognizing that he'd likely live
a longer, less stressful life by
not antagonizing an avenging
Jewish grandma...

...Billy and his henchmen
declined to redraw Barney's
district in a way that would
screw his reelection.

Instead, they gave him
New Bedford.

That summer Barney, Dottie, and a slow-witted intern drove to New Bedford to set up a new district office. It was only sixty miles south of Boston—and just ten from their by now familiar stomping grounds of Fall River. But it seemd farther away nonetheless.

YOU JUST MISSED THE EXIT !

Actually, *I* was the intern. That's how I began to learn the stories in this book

They found an old city hugging the coast like barnacles on the hulls of the battered fishing fleet in its harbor. The three of them parked, then hiked up the windy hill toward town. Clanging from halyards was audible for a good ten minutes before fading from earshot.

Which way?

Um. Left.

Uphill, to the right.

Handsome Victorians, relics of flush whaling days, stood silent vigil next to commercial buildings and antique mariner institutions.

A manufacturing district of mills and factories, just visible at the fringes of a small downtown, streched west for a couple of miles.

Clearly though, the real money was long, long gone. Litter blew through desultory streets. Paint peeled. Addicts swayed on corners.

Dottie, how do I get an outside line?!
Hit 8, then the number.
NINE. Then the number.
Marge, how's business?
Not so fuckin' hot, Dottie. Is he in?
Dottie seemed to know every Bay Stater from the Berkshires to Nantucket.
Get the frigging National Marine Fisheries Service coppers off owah **backs**, Congressman! Pulling fish from the sea is how folks feed their families around here. You put my boats outtah business and this fuckin' town'll just be welfare queens and druggies.
It's them greedy motherfucking Swede boat owners, Congressman. They treat us bad. They lie about the catches. Undercount the fish so they can pay us less. Get the Coast Guard to crack down. You know what I'm sayin'? And hey, for what it's worth, we don't give a fuck about your sex problems, y'know?
You know anything about fish?
Besides preferring Legal Sea Foods to Pier 4? No.
Hire someone who does.
No budget. I can offer our intern.
Groan.
And look into how we can push any economic development, or housing or public safety grants the city may've submitted to the feds.
Will do.
Place needs a lot of help.

SOME TIME LATER

So lately, you've probably been getting these "explanation of benefits" letters in the mail from your health insurance.

Stamped at the top it always says in large letters THIS IS NOT A BILL. Which always makes me want to write back to them and say, "Good, because this is not a check."

But listen, folks, it's important to save these letters, no matter how annoying, because—

What?

....

Sorry, folks, I'm gonna hafta cut this short, unfortunately...

With a thunderclap, the media began reporting news of the president's affair with an intern.

CNN

In fact, though, the seed of scandal had been laid years earlier...

I really like your curves, Mrs. Jones.

Little Rock, 1991

...and had continued to spread intermittently,

Mr. President, here are your papers from, um, the National Security Council, I think...

...right through the president's second term.

And here is a glimpse of my thong.

WHOA! Now that's the kind of special delivery I like!

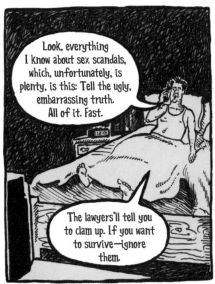

Look, everything I know about sex scandals, which, unfortunately, is plenty, is this: Tell the ugly, embarrassing truth. All of it. Fast.

The lawyers'll tell you to clam up. If you want to survive—ignore them.

So do you think that's what the president is doing?

Hope so.

Thanks for the interview, Congressman.

Sorry, it was WBUR. Got to get right back to these radio reporters. Otherwise they say, "The Congressman wasn't available for comment," which sounds like I'm hiding out at my golf club.

No one thinks Barney Frank is out golfing.

Well, maybe. You still want to have sex?

Not tonight. Got tired.

Oh, ok. G'nite.

He tossed and turned. Good thing Clinton had already been reelected and wouldn't have to face the voters again...

An INTERN!

Consensual?

He said, she said.

Bottom line: They both deny it, him on TV, and her in a deposition in the Paula Jones case. So *proving* the president had an affair is gonna be really hard to do.

HEY GUY WANT A SPOT?

Until Monica anted up proof.

BREAKING NEWS: Miss Lewinsky has handed over to prosecutors a blue dress with the president's DNA.

OY VEY...

He went for lunch. Everywhere, one question reverberated:

How could he be so stupid?

Out of chili?

Barnster!

No mo', grumpy. Howbout bean soup?

Hate the stuff.

A'right. Go ahead an' starve. I do it everyday given the peanuts y'all pay us.

Not looking good, Barn. You see Lieberman's quote?

Sanctimonious SOB.

STUPID.

No arguments there. Still though, getting blown in the Oval? Even JFK wouldn't pull that.

GOT THAT LAST CHILI

Frantic news producers begged prominent Democrats to defend Bill Clinton on camera.

Please!

Please!

PRETTY PLEASE!

None agreed.

Can't tonight.

Really busy.

THE REBBE NACHMAN STORY

Previous engagement.

Except Barney...

Congressman Frank? It's CNN hoping to book you tonight!

I'm on Cape Cod.

We'll send a truck.

Normally the networks demand exclusivity from on-air commentators, but when ABC called, and he said he was already committed to CNN, they just said:

No problem.

8 PM
KEN STARR
Linda Gra
9
BARNE
FR

In rapid succession he fielded calls from the other networks, with the same outcome.

We're booking you.

Booking!

Booking you.

Soon, a fleet of satellite trucks was barreling down Boston's Southeast Expressway, along the Cape's spindly Route 6, and onto the one-lane, bumper-to-drag queen-to-bumper traffic of Provincetown, Mass.

EYEWITNESS 5

On that summer night, talking to the nation from a fundraiser/dinner party in PTown, he was the only important Democrat on the air...

Cheese puffs?

Maybe just one.

I think the American people are smart enough to say...

So exciting! It's history in the making!

...I disapprove of his behavior, which is irresponsible. And of his dishonesty, which is regrettable...but neither rises to the level of an impeachable offense.

And since his economic and political leadership have both been very positive...

...I absolutely DO NOT want him removed from office over an episode of marital infidelity.

...rallying others in support of a progressive presidency (albeit one headed up by a flawed president).

YOU TELL 'EM, BARN'.

Everywhere he went that summer, people reached out appreciatively.

Good job, Congressman!

Love that guy.

Bravo!

Hate that guy.

At home though, his brain trust worried.

You sure it's a good idea to be so public about your support? This guy looks to me like he's going down.

Friendly's

I just can't go along with deep-sixing the most successful Democratic administration since Franklin Roosevelt because he lied about sex.

What about using his power to coerce a young girl into servicing him?

I hear you, Joe, but by her own testimony, she insists it was all consensual.

As consensual as it can be when the girl's an insecure, zaftig twenty-two-year-old, and the boy's the most powerful man on Earth.

Yeah, good point, Elsie.

Don't talk with your mouth full, dear.

Gay Panther

DIVEST

PFLAG

After Labor Day, events quickened. The special prosecutor sent his report to Congress. And Speaker Gingrich immediately called a vote to release it to the public.

445 pages of T.M.I. re: Bill Clinton's Sex Life

STARR REPORT

Early morning in DC a few days later

Phone for you, Barney. Says it's Air Force One!

Well? Lay it on me, brother...

Sorry, Mr. President, but we're gonna lose the vote. The special prosecutor's report will have to be made public.

Why, those disloyal cocksuckers! (No offense, Barney.) They're crucifying me over a couple goddamn blow jobs! After all I've done for them?! When was the last time someone won those motherfuckers a second fuckin' presidential term? Are you fuckin' kidding me!

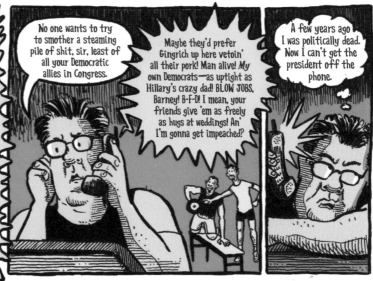

No one wants to try to smother a steaming pile of shit, sir, least of all your Democratic allies in Congress.

Maybe they'd prefer Gingrich up here vetoin' all their pork! Man alive! *My* own Democrats—as uptight as Hillary's crazy dad! BLOW JOBS, Barney! B-F-D! I mean, your friends give 'em as freely as hugs at weddings! An' I'm gonna get impeached?

A few years ago I was politically dead. Now I can't get the president off the phone.

A week later video of the president's humiliating grand jury appearance was released.

I had a sexual involvement when I said I hadn't. I lied to protect my family.

Congressional Republicans were certain they now had the public support to force Clinton from office and to sweep the mid-term elections that November.

Democrats, on the other hand, were petrified, certain that furious voters would soon eject anyone supporting the horndog sitting in the Oval Office.

ON SHIT ON SHIT ON SHIT

A funny thing happened, though, on the way to the Democrats' electoral catastrophe...

YEAH!

It didn't happen.

Gallup and CNN tracked the president's approval hovering at around 60%—a little bit higher, even.

Watching the president be grilled by prosecutors, not about corruption, or abuse of office, but about what they saw as an extramarital affair, caused many Americans to identify...

Y'know what? So what.

News that shocked in January (he did WHAT with his cigar?) had become humdrum by September.

Awright, so he's tacky, and we wouldn't let our daughter date him. But he's also a halfway decent president. Cares about us. We're employed.

And despite the embarrassing revelations in November, the Democrats swept the midterms.

What's the tally?

We're WAY up.

DISTRICT OFFICE US CONGRESS

But the Republicans pushed on by voting to authorize the House Judiciary Committee to begin impeachment hearings...

Don't stop thinkin' about tomorrow..

You said he'd be **dead** by now, **Newt!**

Curse you, Bill Clinton! CURSE you!

Days later, the House Judiciary Committee convened.

The first witness was Special Prosecutor Kenneth Starr, who read an opening statement glossing over certain trumped-up allegations in order to get quickly to the sexy stuff.

CONSPIRACY CRAP ABOUT THE DEATH OF VINCE FOSTER

OFFICE OF THE SPECIAL PROSECUTOR INVESTIGATION INTO TRAVELGATE

OFFICE OF THE SPECIAL PROSECUTOR INVESTIGATION INTO FILEGATE

The special prosecutor was obsessive—think Inspector Javert, from Victor Hugo's *Les Misérables*.

We do not anticipate that evidence gathered in the Travelgate, or Filegate, or Vince Fostergate investigations will be relevant to this committee's impeachment deliberations. The president was not involved. Turning to matters of *fellatio*—

Wait...WHAT?

Which offered Barney, the lead Democrat on the impeachment panel (John Conyers was more senior, but getting up in years), an opportunity to expose the special prosecutor's porterhouse-thick hypocrisy.

Waitaminute, Mr. Starr, when did you conclude there was no information incriminating the president in these other investigations?

Ahem, some time ago.

So you pushed to make public the embarrassing details about President Clinton and Ms. Lewinsky before the election, but withheld exoneration of the president for Filegate and Travelgate.

Starr mumbled a nonanswer to Barney in legalese, but the truth was clear to anyone paying attention: he'd hoped to sway the midterms.

A few days later, the House voted to impeach the president on just two of eleven counts of lying about Monica in the deposition for the Paula Jones lawsuit.

Adjourned, thank God.

And in that way, nearly dead on arrival,

articles of impeachment were sent to the Senate.

Which dispatched them quickly by voting to acquit the president.

And so with a whimper, not a bang, the drama concluded.

Bill Clinton was grateful. He flew up to Massachusetts to publicly thank Barney for helping to save his ass...

...and the only two-term Democratic presidency in forty years.

There's no one I'd rather have by my side in an all-out brawl. You all should feel the same about your congressman.

But if the political dividend he'd earned was considerable, so was the cost.

GREAT JOB, CONGRESSMAN!

I'm home.

Herb?

Herbie? You here?

Dear Barney—
That old line about "Washington being a town of powerful men and the wives they married when they were younger"?
Sorry. Just Not who I want to be.
—Herb

OH, you're home.

Yeah. I live here. I thought you did too.

Sorry. I thought you'd be up in Mass.

That Saturday, Herb returned to take his things. He brought a new friend with him.

Herb seemed nervous and remote. The friend seemed disdainful. Both seemed way younger than he felt. They had on matching muscle shirts.

With the last load, Herb called from the front:

Uh, Barney, *we're* headed out.

The locks clicked, he heard the keys tumble through the mail slot.

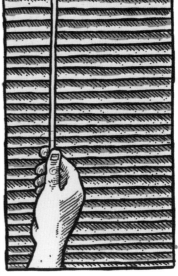

25.
The
Ugly
Aughts

In the 2006 midterm election, five years after 9/11, and three after we punched a hole in Iraq...

...American voters lost faith that President George W. Bush and his gang of neocons had any clue about what they were doing.

Mr. President, about Scooter Libby—

Not now, Dick, watchin' my best show!

Har!

Democrats took control of the House, elevating Barney to the chairmanship of the powerful Financial Services Committee...

I'm open to working with you Republicans on affordable housing.

Don't hold your breath.

...just as it was becoming clear that something was very screwed up about Wall Street, and by extension, our whole economy.

C'mon, aren't these foreclosures happening because all these idiots bought too much house?

Uh-uh. A lot of 'em got suckered. Low interest rate to start, balloon rate kicks in later.

So really, you're saying they didn't read their own goddamn mortgages.

Hidden in the fine print. On purpose. And offered to buyers the broker *knew* wouldn't be able to make the payments.

The minute a broker collected his fee from one of these predatory sales, he sold the shitty loan—together with more like them—to somebody else.

Hold on! I thought you wanted **more homeownership!** But now you're criticizing easier lending! Isn't that what made more homeownership possible in the first place?

Bullshit. I want lenders to give lower-income people a fairer shake when they apply for a mortgage. That's a lot different from scamming them into buying a house they can't afford.

You want me to fold that paper, boss?

NO.

Hell, we've been trying to get more responsibility in lending for years. Passed a bill in '94 giving the Fed all this power to crack down on shady lenders, but **Alan Greenspan,** like the crazy friggin' Oracle of Delphi, just said:

THE MARKET WILL POLICE ITSELF.

In 2005 we were in the minority, but we joined with more reasonable folks on the other side to tighten lending and to rein in the big companies that buy up all the home loans...

So what happened?

Tom DeLay and the other zealots in the Republican leadership read the riot act to the Republicans on our committee who were working with us. Our bipartisan bill was strangled in its crib.

Night, fellas.

History lessons in gay dives aside, it was a busy time.

Congressman!

His job as chairman of a powerful committee involved making sure that allies held on to their seats in tough districts around the country. A guy couldn't pass progressive legislation if he didn't have the votes.

A word, please!

Colleagues often asked him to headline their fundraisers. He tried always to agree...

It would be just soooo swell if you'd come.

Sure, Tom.

...no matter how ballbusting it was on him or his staff.

Just ran into the representative from Maine's 2nd. Wants me to come up this weekend for a thing.

Oh, NO PROBLEM. I'll just shoehorn it between your eighty other meetings this weekend. But first, let me solve North Korea's nuke issue.

Which is why, on one particular weekend in 2006, he found himelf up in Portland, Maine, waiting for a volunteer to drive him to a speaking gig.

JETPORT

HONK IF YOU LOVE WICCANS

RAINBOWS HAPPEN

MY PUG FOR PRESIDENT!

It was one of a great many trips he was now doing annually. Making a quick speech, endorsing a candidate, answering policy questions, and cracking up his audiences...

I have this fear that one day there's gonna be a fire in the Senate. And tragically, they'll all perish, because they won't have the votes to allow themselves to leave the building.

MAINE DEMS

ME, 2nd DISTRICT DEMS

YOU THE MAN!

An hour later, obligation fulfilled, he scanned the crowd for his driver.

Just ask him. Just ask him. Just ask him.

Why do they always vanish when I want to go?

If he was lucky, he'd catch an earlier flight, get a decent night's sleep for a change, and maybe get breakfast and the papers in Newton before—

hustling down to New Bedford for another Sunday schedule packed within an inch of its life.

FRESH CUP BRAH?

DOW SLIDES MORE WAY MORE

SO MUCH FOR THIS FANTASY

LIKE [EXTRA] UNBEFUCKIN' BELIEVABLY MORE...

Excuse me, Congressman Frank?

Thank you soooooo much for that AMAZING talk! We are such fans of you up here! OH MY GOD! I always catch you on Rachel Maddow. Like without fail!

POOFtttt

And I hate to impose on you, for just a sec? But the thing is, Congressman, there's this **other fundraiser**, just down the coast, starts in about an hour...

I, uh, planned on getting right back to Bos— What's the event for?

Fighting a referendum to overturn the state legislature's inclusion of sexual orientation in Maine's civil rights law.

Do you want to reject the state law that protects people in Maine from discrimination in employment, public accommodation, and credit based on sexual orientation?

OK, you're driving. And we leave now.

OH MY GOSH. Awesomesauce! Can I just grab a few friends for a group picture before we head out?

No. Where's your car?

An hour later he found himself dockside in Ogunquit, Maine. He'd heard it was a gay resort town, though he'd never been before. It seemed nice, without the Cape's whiff of preppy anti-Semitism or the designer pretentiousness of Fire Island.

Ta *da*!

He wolfed down a plate of cheese and crackers...

Don't they feed you in Washington, Congressman?

Ignore her! Welcome to Ogunquit.

...then stood up to speak before an appreciative crowd.

I want LGBT people to have the right to marry, serve in the military, and enjoy the right to a job based solely on our qualifications. I acknowledge that this is an **agenda**...

...but I don't think any self-respecting radical in history would consider advocating for people's right to get married, serve in the military, and earn a living as a terribly revolutionary platform.

He never thought of himself as an orator. Not with his raspy voice and Jersey diction. But the crowd's reaction was so warm that for a moment, he felt like Teddy or Jesse or Barbara Jordan. It was moving to be around LGBT people in more out-of-the-way places. Their need for justice seemed even more urgent than it was in the rest of America.

Thanks very much.

Ninety minutes later, though, he was spent. They called him a cab and he waited by the curb, fiddling with a flip phone, unable to pick up messages due to the lousy reception.

Someone tapped his shoulder.

Can't tell you how good it is to see you again after all these years, Congressman. Not sure I'll get another chance.

An older man, wan looking, though his smile was bright. He wore layers of clothing despite the warm night.

A strong-looking younger guy gripped his left arm, while he, the older guy, extended his right.

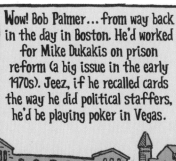

Bob Palmer, Barney. Been a long time.

Wow! Bob Palmer... from way back in the day in Boston. He'd worked for Mike Dukakis on prison reform (a big issue in the early 1970s). Jeez, if he recalled cards the way he did political staffers, he'd be playing poker in Vegas.

ATTICA, 1971

BOB PALMER! Wow, how nice to see you!

They caught up for a few minutes...

He was always running into people he was truly glad to see but too tired and pressed to spend time with—but Palmer was talking about Kevin, and so few people brought the mayor up anymore.

The younger guy was wearing shorts. Hard not to notice that he had a cute butt.

Getting chilly out here. If you're gonna talk, lemme zip you up.

And this is my partner, Jim. Apparently he's had something of a crush on you, which I learned about only yesterday when we saw a poster mentioning you'd be in Portland.

Since he was a teenager! He saw you on Boston TV when you first came out! So you were a role model! Well, I told Jim that I knew—or used to know—you personally!

Right, Jim?

Yeah. Thought you were a pretty brave dude for coming out back then.

Sorta bear-ish, 'n' handsome too.

Anyway, Bobby, we probably shouldn't hold up the representative any longah.

OH-UH. My taxi won't be here for a few minutes.

HONK

We got a call from our trusty LGBT phone tree just a few hours ago saying Barney Frank might show up in town! And I thought *"Hell, let's go see him, I bet he and my Jim would get on well!"*

Palmer kept grinning. Barney felt weirdly like he was being set up on a blind date—one that wasn't so blind given that Jim was standing here, hearing every word.

A sighted date?

Well, uh, sure. I'd love to get together sometime. There's a couple of tight house races, so I'll be back this way before November. Give me your number so I have it.

A few weeks later he called. The number he'd been given was Jim's cell. That had been two years ago.

Bob & Jim
(902) 555-1306

A discreet thing between the two of them developed.

Hey, watching the news and eating dinner. Beef and broccoli, and brown rice, but I'm trying not to eat all the rice. T-shirt and sweats...I miss you

Near the end of Palmer's life, Jim asked Barney up to Maine for a bedside visit.

So Mayor James Michael Curley is standing on the hood of his enormous car, speaking before a huge crowd in West Roxbury, and he's waxing eloquent about charity and the poor. But then he sees an arm reach into the back seat of the convertible and he drops the highfalutin tone and yells, **"That bastard's stealing my goddamn fur coat."**

They regaled each other with war stories.

No clue what you two are going on about, but glad you're having fun.

HA HA HA!

Palmer passed away. Barney and Jim spent more time together up in Maine.

And in DC.

HEYA Mister chairman! Can you spare a quick minute to talk about payday lenders?

Call my office for an appointment.

Won't take but a sec!

Hey, Gucci Gulch. *Beat it.*

26. Meltdown.

Years of the government turning a blind eye to predatory, irresponsible (and sometimes illegal) behavior on Wall Street and in the mortgage industry...

...led to a housing bubble, its bursting, and the Great Recession that followed.

As chairman of the House Financial Services committee, Barney developed a good working relationship with the Republican secretary of the Treasury, Henry Paulson...

What you need to understand about the scallop fishery, Congressman, is this—

Sorry to interrupt, Barney. Secretary Paulson is on the line.

... who got in the habit of calling on Friday afternoons, when Barney was back in Massachusetts meeting with constituents...

Yes, Mr. Secretary?

WORRYINGLY, New Century and American Home Mortgages have both filed for bankruptcy.

...or grabbing an hour of downtime in Ogunquit before hopping on a flight back to DC or wherever else.

It's your other new boyfriend, Hank.

Distressing news, Chairman. Fitch has downgraded Countrywide's rating. Oh, and Bear Stearns was gonna go bust, so we got the Fed to backstop $30 billion of its debt.

$30 million, you mean.

No. Billion.

A Few Weeks Later

Barney? Hank. Just giving you a heads-up that the Treasury just fired the leadership of Fannie Mae and Freddie Mac and placed both of them in receivership. Also...

Merrill Lynch is gonna go bust unless we find a really rich buyer.

If Paulson was increasingly troubled about the state of the economy in late 2008, his fellow Republicans in Congress didn't seem to share his concerns.

Hard-line, right wing US House Majority Leader Tom DeLay

Over our dead body will the gov'mint bail out any of these godless banks.

I've spent the past month trying to cobble together some solution for Lehman Brothers that doesn't involve a federal bailout. Nothing works. The markets are tanking. Wealth is being wiped out across the country. People will lose their homes, their savings, and their jobs if we do nothing.

SEC. PAULSON

A million more foreclosures? 80% unemployment? Poor folks roasting rats over garbage can fires in the streets? That's *Capitalism*, baby. Do I make myself clear?

In addition to his day job, Majority Leader DeLay wound up a contestant on *Dancing with the Stars*. (Not super relevant to our story but sufficiently gross to include nonetheless.)

Hey, Jim? It's Peter, from Barney's office. Sorry to wake you. Secretary Paulson's looking for him. They're meeting in Senator Reid's office in an hour. Treasury's sending a car.

Seventy-five minutes later Barney and other sleep-deprived officials convened at the Senate majority leader's office. Speaker Nancy Pelosi, looking impeccable, tightly wound, and gimlet-eyed as usual, said:

You wanted to meet with us, Mr. Secretary? Something about your Wall Street friends having ruined the American economy?

(sigh) Thank you, Madam Speaker. I'll cut to the chase. A company you may not know, AIG, has become the linchpin of the global financial system.

You see, the big Wall Street banks each have a certain type of contract with AIG, called a **credit default swap.** Basically, AIG insures the banks against loss if the debt they hold, in the form of bundles of shady mortgages, for example, goes south.
BEN BERNANKE FEDERAL RESERVE CHAIRMAN
Problem is, that's exactly what's happened. All of the banks took on bad debt, and AIG doesn't have the cash to pay out on their policies. AIG fails, the biggest banks will fail also, and our economy will tank.
So what we are going to do is this: Ben here will advance AIG $85 billion, in the hopes of forestalling an economic meltdown.
BED HEAD SITUATION
Wait. WHAT? Where did you get $85 billion?
The Federal Reserve has **$850 billion in reserves,** actually. Not that I'm keen on spending it.
So lemme get this straight: All week, the Bush administration and its allies in Congress have refused to bail out banks, because doing so would constitute a sacrilegious intervention in the functioning of the free market. But tonight you're championing an $85 billion bailout for some insurance company?
WHAT IN THE HELL'S CHANGED?
Easy answer, Mr. Chairman. The galloping hooves of economic apocalypse got closer.

The next day they met again.

That $85 billion for AIG isn't cutting it.

There's going to have to be a much more significant intervention into the financial sector in order to save the economy from complete collapse.

How much "more," exactly, Mr. Secretary?

$700 billion from Congress. By tomorrow, please.

HAW!

Then Ben Bernanke explained the Bush administration's latest bailout proposal—called TARP for entirely forgettable reasons.

The federal government will use the $700B to buy up all the toxic home loans held by America's banks, to help them limit their losses so they can start lending again.

They might have called the plan SCARED SHITLESS, because by the end of the meeting—after an hour of Paulson's and Bernanke's dire predictions—that's what everybody was.

Wait, you're serious about that $700 billion?

Entirely.

CRACK

Speaker Pelosi assigned Barney the hopeless task of persuading House members to support the Bush administration's ginormous bailout.

Will do.

But it fast became clear that many of the House Democrats,

as well as most of the House Republicans, were not about to cooperate across the aisle voluntarily.

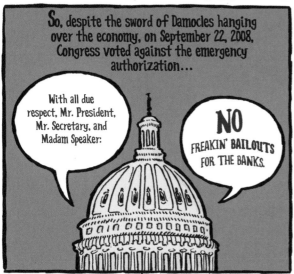

So, despite the sword of Damocles hanging over the economy, on September 22, 2008, Congress voted against the emergency authorization...

With all due respect, Mr. President, Mr. Secretary, and Madam Speaker:

NO FREAKIN' BAILOUTS FOR THE BANKS.

...and in response, the Dow promptly fell 777 points.

So a third emergency meeting was held, this time with President Bush, the Congressional leadership, and presidential candidates Senators McCain and Obama. Barney knew more about financial legislation than most of the others, and he repeatedly violated protocol by speaking without being called upon by W.

Look, Hank, and uh, Mr. President, NO WAY are you getting the Democratic votes you need on any TARP re-vote...

Panel 1: ...unless you include foreclosure relief for **underwater homeowners...**

Agreed, mi pushy gay hombre. Hank, add the foreclosure stuff for homeowners *under the agua.* An' now all you cowpokes, this meetin's adjourned.

Panel 2: But the president, with only a few months remaining in his term, didn't seem to mind.

Panel 3: So, Congress held another vote on TARP. This time, spooked by the Dow's free fall, they passed it.

Well, the ayes have it. We've done the responsible thing. Unlike the Gordon Gekko idiots who got us into this mess.

Panel 4: Three weeks later, Barack Obama was elected president. It was a watershed moment for the USA.

Panel 5: But the foreclosures didn't take a coffee break for history. The crisis of Americans losing their homes only accelerated.

Panel 6: Federal TARP dollars—now available because Congress had acted—were doled out in two pots, the first of which was quickly emptied to stabilize the nation's largest banks...

Panel 7: ...with nothing spent to help homeowners about to lose their houses.

Grass is gettin' a little long. *Just sayin'.* Hey, you folks know if this is the way to the Hamptons heliport?

Panel 8: Infuriated, Barney called a new hearing and summoned Secretary Paulson to the hot seat.

You've already tapped TARP for an astronomical $370 billion without spending a cent on the homeowner relief that Democratic support for the bailout was predicated on!

Panel 9: The Treasury will include homeowner relief in the second tranche of TARP funding. But only if incoming President-Elect Obama asks us to do it.

But the president-elect sidestepped the mess for as long as he could.

I don't take the oath until January. One president at a time, folks.

Barack's really overstating the number of presidents we currently have.

CAM CRAWFORD TEXAS

Hoo boy, think I just run over a rattler!

Because it was rushed into law during an emergency, TARP offered a rare chance to get debt relief for homeowners past Congress's free-market zealots.

A BILL

Once the emergency passed though, so did the opportunity.

We pay our mortgage. Why should our taxpayer dollars go to help a bunch of DEADBEATS who don't?

Damn right.

I guess no one ever claimed America's motto is *mi casa es su casa.* Ain't that right, pooch? Heheheheh.

A month later, in January '09, Barack Obama was inaugurated—

GASP! Oh my gosh, Barney, he's headed right for us!

I'll introduce you.

and immediately became responsible for an imploding economy.

Congratulations, Mr. President. It's a good day. Though if you'll forgive me for saying so, I think you made a bad call on foreclosure relief.

Nice to meet you, Jim. Listen, you gonna help me keep your boyfriend under control over the next four years?

YESSIR!

I'm gonna start with health care, but then we're gonna need a Wall Street bill. So roll up your sleeves.

Consider them rolled, sir.

Signs of the crash were everywhere: long lines at government benefits offices, constituent after constituent wanting him to intercede with banks or collection agencies...

A lot of his time was spent trying to help constituents avoid foreclosure...

Dottie, call Countrywide and say Congressman Frank would like to inquire about modifying Mr. Silva's mortgage.

Will call now.

Dottie, call Washington Mutual and tell them Congressman Frank wants to know what we can do to modify Mrs. White's mortgage.

Yup, calling.

Dottie, call Wachovia and say Congressman Frank would like to inquire about options for modifying the Toughys' mortgage.

On it.

And on the phone with Paulson arguing about executive pay.

These modern-day Marie Antoinettes are cutting themselves obscene paychecks while driving their companies into the ground.

If the government starts telling them what they can't do regarding executive compensation, they'll pull out of TARP and take the economy down with them.

Scoundrels!

GALLATIN

Mr. Secretary, I can't think of a more damning indictment of the CEO class in this country.

It is what it is, Mr. Chairman.

Rather insanely, a month later AIG accepted $173 billion in bailout money, then awarded fat bonuses to its failed executives.

THE WALL STREET JOURNAL
AIG TO PAY MILLIONS TO THOSE WHO CAUSED MELTDOWN

We should claw back the bonuses!

We can't, Senator Dodd. Even though the bailout money came from the federal government, the bonuses came from AIG as a contract between the company and its employees.

And the government has no power to break a legal contract between a company and its employees.

Right.

Even when the government is propping the company up with billions of taxpayer dollars?! How can that be right? Could we tax the bonuses at, I dunno, 95 percent?

We'd need an act of Congress for that. And we don't have the votes. No Republican is going to vote for a confiscatory tax.

Without a better idea on the table, he called another hearing, hauled AIG's new CEO to the witness stand, and became a vessel for the public's howling anger...

I insist, under threat of subpoena,

that you immediately provide this committee with the names and addresses of each AIG employee receiving one of these obscene bonuses.

It was a spontaneous and not-well-thought-out demand. His committee staffers were appalled.

Vigilantism.

Potential for violence.

Bad policy.

Oh no, with all due respect, Chairman Frank, there have already been death threats against some of our people!

The hearing ended and he let the matter drop—deciding that demagoguing wasn't a solution for the millions of people losing their homes, jobs, and savings due to the chicanery of Wall Street wiseguys.

You should'a stuck to your guns, Barney!

Not now, Maxine.

By the end of the year, the destruction they had wrought was really awesome to behold.

Falls under your jurisdiction. Get it fixed. Chop chop.

Yes, Madam Speaker.

8.7 Million jobs lost. $19 Trillion in household wealth lost. 4 Million foreclosures.

We need to insist that banks hold on to a portion of the debt so that they have an incentive to sell mortgages only to people who can make payments.

SKIN IN THE GAME.

Exactly.

Good. I like it. Draft it up.

He also wanted to crack down on subprime lending practices that had fueled the housing bubble using shady mortgage products with names like:

The Hustle

FAST 'N' EASY

So you're saying we can get this place for almost nothing down?

And then we can refinance later on better terms?

Givin' you my word, folks. Chance of a lifetime! Don't be the poor schmucks who miss out! You deserve a beautiful home!

But these mortgages were laden with hidden fees, penalties, and fat commissions for brokers, who lured buyers with easy credit—

coupled with adjustable rates that ballooned after a few years.

Consumer advocates, public interest attorneys, and academics all weighed in with Barney and his staff about about how to stop the mortgage scamming...

POP
POP
POP.
POP

...as well as the stacked-against-the-consumer decks that were the credit card, auto loan, and payday lending industries.

FINE PRINT

PAY DAY

C'mon down!

A Harvard Law School professor named Elizabeth Warren spoke out in favor of creating a a new federal consumer finance watchdog agency:

In America, it's impossible to buy a toaster that has a one-in-five chance of bursting into flames and burning your house down.

But incredibly, it's absolutely possible to get a mortgage that has the same one-in-five chance of putting your family out on the street. And that mortgage won't even contain a disclosure of that fact to the consumer. It's just plain wrong and we need to do something about it!

Barney agreed with her, and decided to make creation of a national Consumer Financial Protection Bureau a centerpiece of the reform bill...

Good!

Title 10.
"Creation of the New Bureau."

...but he knew it would never pass if America's bankers united in their opposition.

Segel had come down from Boston to serve as committee counsel.

No way are we gonna conquer unless we divide.

Agreed. set up a meeting with the small banks.

The Independent Community Bankers of America (ICBA) is a trade group of small and midsize banks across the USA.

They lack Wall Street's wealth, but make up for it in political clout, with lobbyists in every state house and city hall.

Camden Fine was ICBA's chief.

Hello, Mr. Fine, please go on in.

Look, Cam, we know *your* banks have been doing their job of funding small businesses and weren't in on the subprime lending, or any of the other noxious features that dug us this giant shithole.

What I want to know is, what would it take for the country's small banks to not oppose our effort to **dig us out?**

Well, Mr. Chairman, we oppose your new Consumer Financial Protection Bureau, because our banks can't handle yet another government regulator waltzing in and subjecting us to another excruciating examination of our books. We're up the wazoo with regulators examining our books.

What if we exempted small and midsize banks from the new bureau's examination?

Really?

I don't have all day, Cam.

Not what I expected the Great Liberal Ogre to propose, Mr. Chairman. Throw in a change to the formula requiring big banks to pay their fair share for federal deposit insurance, and, well, sir, you've gotta deal.

OK, another brain-twisting subject: our approach to derivatives?

So, banks are using these contracts, which are based on the value of some underlying commodity like corn, or oil, **or in our case mortgages,** as a hedge against losses.

Huge bundles of subprime mortgages have been converted into securities, which are being traded on what's become a trillion-dollar derivatives market.

Problem being, this new market's totally unregulated, and people don't really know the value of what's being traded. That's why Warren Buffett calls derivatives—

WEAPONS OF MASS FINANCIAL DESTRUCTION!

Even so, they're being swapped at a furious rate, without the traders knowing how much they're worth. They're like this contagion of debt, stemming from investment in these huge bundles of bad mortgages.

Hmm. I'm still not clear how all this works.

Neither are the hotshots doing the trading. That's why AIG has become one of the biggest deadbeats in history.

So, what are we going to do about it?
To reduce the risk of exposure, and to improve the transparency of prices and of who owes what to whom, we'll require that all trades go through a central clearinghouse.
And that'll work?
Jesus, let's hope so.
OK, what else?
Ending TOO BIG TO FAIL banks, by giving the US Treasury the authority to shut banks down if they pose a risk to the entire financial system.
STAFF H
DRAFT
DRAFT
DRAF
And the cost for unwinding them will come from their own capital reserves that we'll demand they beef up, and a special annual assessment.
DRAFT
NO, say it more plainly. Right in the text of the bill. NO MORE TAXPAYER BAILOUTS for failing banks.
Hey, any idea what's happening *over there?*
The Senate.
Who the fuck knows.
SHIVER

27.
Sausage
Factory

A Few Days Later

Hold on, lemme fix your collar.

Look, Barney, we'll never get Wall Street reform through Congress unless I give Republican senators a chance to weigh in constructively.

Sigh. Fine, Chris, but will they?

Sorry, Senator, but I think that's wishful bullshit.

I think the Republicans on my committee are interested in working with us on Wall Street reform in a spirit of bipartisanship.

Yeah, I think they're just going to pretend to be interested while they wait for an opening to scuttle the whole deal.

Don't water down the bill to placate them because—I learned this with health care—they'll never be satisfied.

Later, back at Rayburn

OK, what else?

We need to crack down on the rating agencies.

Fitch, Standard & Poor's, and Moody's all continue to mindlessly rubber-stamp "TRIPLE A" on every goddamn toxic mortgage-backed security put in front of them.

Why, for God's sake?

Because they convinced themselves that home prices would would rise forever; consequently, triple A ratings for everyone!

Volkswagens with cheating emissions standards? **Triple A.** Intelligence about Saddam's WMD? **Triple A.** Health of my uncle Mort, who passed three years ago? goddamn **triple A.**

And by rating securitized mortgages that were clearly pieces of shite, they fanned the flames of binge trading.

OK, we crack down on the rating agencies. What else?

The White House likes Paul Volcker's proposal to ban banks from trading with their depositors' money.

Fine. Get the language in our bill.

Also, maybe this is the time to do something with a more international reach. How about that blood diamond issue? Can we require all US corporations to certify that every dollar they spend overseas on resource extraction was done legally?

I'll get you a draft by tonight.

Problem with some of the Dem moderates on our committee: they want to exempt auto loans from the oversight of our proposed Consumer Financial Protection Bureau.

Shit. God knows it's an area of abuse...

I've probably bought and driven more lemons than the rest of you combined. Segel drives a rental here in DC, but he probably tools around Brookline in a Bentley convertible...

Guilty.

But everyone likes their local dealership—the folks with the terrible TV ads who sponsor your kid's Little League team. If we can stem exemptions to the new bureau's oversight to small banks and auto loans, we might have to accept those limitations.

Meanwhile, Republicans insisted that the effort to reform an out-of-control financial sector was—

The result of a diabolical Democrat plot to expand homeownership and also—

Job-KILLING socialist overreach!

Senate Republicans House Republicans

In December 2009, after months of hard work (and a last-minute threat by the Congressional Black Caucus to withhold support), Barney's Wall Street reform bill was passed by the House.

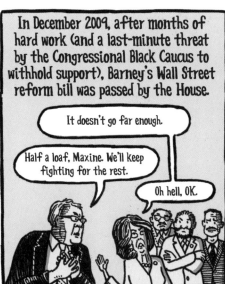

It doesn't go far enough.

Half a loaf, Maxine. We'll keep fighting for the rest.

Oh hell, OK.

But over in the Senate, Wall Street reform wasn't moving...

Sunnuvabitch

...until that august body became aware of something called **Abacus.**

Wall Street firm Goldman Sachs had been pushing this Abacus—a mortgage-backed security—to its clients.

This baby'll grow your portfolio. Trust me!

The prospectus seems to smell a bit.

Oh, tut-tut. What fertilizer doesn't? You really should **BUY.** Will you excuse me just a moment?

SELL!

Pissed about Goldman's Abacus scam, the Senate finally passed its own reform.

Now the two versions, House and Senate, would need to be reconciled so a final bill could be sent to the president.

Conference committee?

Looks that way.

Basically we've got the House side sewn up. It sucks that we don't have any Republican votes, but we'll win anyway.

It's the other side that worries me.

With their margin so tight over there, every goddamn member of the Senate can play God.

GRUNT.

Not long after, he led a House delegation over to the Senate to hash out their policy differences.

NOK NOK

Representatives from the Lesser House approacheth.

GREETINGS, PLEBEIANS!

Getta load'a this shit.

At the conference committee...

...they quickly got down to business. Staff hovered over members, offering revised amendments, compromise language, expert advice. Noisy monster floor fans supplemented the Dirksen Building's shitty AC, which old-timers muttered had never been up to the task of a July heat wave in the capital.

From spectator seats provided grudgingly by Senate clerks, banking lobbyists in their smart summer seersucker...

...and consumer advocates in the same suits they wore year-round kept close watch over every move made by the conferees...

...taking mostly party-line votes on each.

As predicted, the conference meant sidebar negotiations with one senatorial ego after another.

My donors say let the banks gamble with SOME of their customers' deposits.

Senator
Scottius Brownius

Nay, my donors say exclude banks from the deriatives market unless a *Push-Out Provision* is added.

Huh?

Got me.

Senator Blanchus
Lincolnus

We will vote for final passage, giving your bill a critically needed bipartisan patina. But only if you kill the annual assessment on banks to fund these reforms.

Senators from
DownEastius

So the **taxpayers**, not the **fat cats**, will have to foot the bill for cleaning up the mess made by Wall Street?

Alas, yes.

As a House-Senate compromise draft labored toward passage, a snag developed concerning the virginity of Senator Russ Feingoldeanus.

I cannot vote for it, as it is less perfectly progressive than I.

Eventually, and exhaustingly, on the third day of the conference—well, technically the fourth, since it was the middle of the night—the compromise draft passed. Which meant that, against all odds...

...they'd managed to pass landmark, pro-consumer legislation through one of the most polarized Congresses in history.

The **ayes** have it.

He allowed himself, for just a moment, to imagine LBJ clamping a congratulatory paw on his shoulder.

And thought of Tip...

...lumbering over to some celestial drinks trolley to pour them each a glass of Madeira.

Proud of you, Bahney. Your bill's gonna change people's lives for the bettah. And isn't that why we got into this shitty business in the first place?

Actually, someone in the conference room did pop a bottle of champagne. But mostly everyone was too exhausted and hot to linger. Even the reporters—the *Journal*, CNBC, *Bloomberg*—were too spent for interviews.

A few days later, POTUS sent a fancy bus to take them down Pennsylvania Avenue to the White House for a bill signing ceremony.

The Republicans boycotted. With a few exceptions, they hadn't voted for the bill, though they magnanimously agreed to name it after Barney and Senator Dodd.

We don't want *our* name on the damn thing.

THE DODD-FRANK WALL STREET REFORM and CONSUMER PROTECTION ACT OF 2010

We'd never get another donation.

And within a few minutes, the president had signed it into law.

Then Congress recessed for the summer.

HEY!

Barney headed up to Massachusetts. On his way, rushing through Reagan National, he was recognized by a group of tourists from Hangzhou...

Hey! Isn't that Barney Frank Dodd?

Who?

Frank Dodd, American bank honcho!

Ni hao!

Hey, Frank Dodd! We need a bailout too. Hahaha.

Was this how he was perceived out there? Frank Dodd the Big Bailout Chief? Of course, these were Chinese tourists, not voters in Brookline or New Bedford. But still. He tried to put the worrying notion out of his head.

Bye-bye, Frank Dodd.

Many politicians enjoy the glad-handing of politics, but shy away from the wonkish details of governing. For him, though, it had always been the other way around.

Anyone who says they love campaigning is either crazy or a liar.

YAWN. Yawn.

Nevertheless, you need to be at Coolidge Corner T station at 7 AM. And here's the rest of tomorrow's schedule.

Even in progressive Brookline, there were people standing in traffic waving signs for his opponent—

TEA PARTY

NO BAILOUT$

SHAME ON YOU BARNEY!

a square-jawed, jug-eared ex-Marine from upstate New York nobody had ever heard of a few months earlier, but who was now rolling in Tea Party dough.

SEAN BIELAT CONGRESS

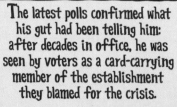
The latest polls confirmed what his gut had been telling him: after decades in office, he was seen by voters as a card-carrying member of the establishment they blamed for the crisis.

What's it say?

Nuthin' good.

POLS

Jim was new to all this. It was his first campaign as the openly gay boyfriend of an openly gay congressman.

TEA PARTY!

NO BAIL OUTS

DUMP FRANK

He found a niche, though, as the campaign videographer. At least until he caught flak for recording Barney's opponent without permission.

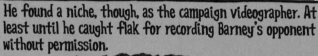

Sir, you're with the Frank campaign, correct? Please do not take videos.

Our campaign would be happy to provide you with authorized images.

It's a free country, dude.

EXIT

WGBH

Not until we TAKE THIS COUNTRY BACK! Heh heh heh.

Lame joke, dude. Don't quit your day job.

Seriously? You're heckling me on camera?

A clip of this embarrassing exchange between the congressman's boyfriend and his opponent went viral.

Oh brother.

Lame joke, dude.
Lame joke, dude.
Lake joke, dude.

His brain trust groaned and wrung their hands. But he felt differently.

This is a PR nightma— wait, Barney, are you actually *smiling?*

Never had an overzealous spouse to defend me in public. It's a nice feeling.

The 2010 midterm voters were in an unforgiving mood. In the end, he eked out his own reelection, but Tea Party Republicans took the House—so he lost his chairmanship, and the staff and perks that came with it. He'd never given a damn about perks, but it was very painful that many of the staffers who'd worked so hard on Dodd-Frank would now get pink slips instead of raises.

And then, another blow: Beacon Hill unveiled its new congressional redistricting map for 2012.

What about Bahney?

He'll be OK. He always is.

And they screwed him.

Shit, they took New Bedford out of your district and gave you towns way out west in *Worcester County*, ferchrissakes. Might as well be Pennsylvania.

So I've totaled it up: 40 percent of this new district is people you've never represented. And it's as Republican a district as you're gonna find in Massachusetts. You'll win again, but we'll have to rehash all of it. Even Gobie.

He still felt plenty of fight. But up at Jim's house in Maine over a long weekend, something occurred to him.

This is so nice. I could sit here all day just listening to him snore.

It was a strange feeling for life to be offering a refuge from work and not the other way around.

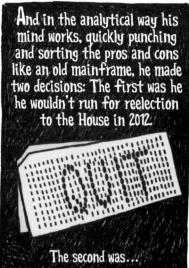

And in the analytical way his mind works, quickly punching and sorting the pros and cons like an old mainframe, he made two decisions: The first was he wouldn't run for reelection to the House in 2012.

QUIT

The second was...

Hey, Jim?

(sleepily) Huh, yeah?

Will you marry me?

I love you, so yeah. I'll marry you.

28. Dancing.

The wedding was on the banks of the Charles. One of those hazy July days that refuses to promise either sunshine or rain. The sort of day that reminds New Englanders, by birth or by choice, who they are, and of all who've come before them—abolitionists, Narragansett sachems, irascible presidents, captains of industry and clipper ships, brewers, Freedom Riders—iconoclasts of every stripe who've loved this stubborn landscape.

The famous mingled warmly with the not-so-famous…

From the Dunkin' at Pahk Street. How do you know him?

…bound by their newfound affection for Jim–this man who was making their old friend so happy at last…

…and by their love for Barney, of whom they had now spent much of their lives saying:

You *gotta* love Barney Frank to like him.

The governor married them in a very pretty ceremony. They kissed and everyone cheered.

Some guests, though–those with years ahead as combatants in an ongoing struggle for a more progressive world–

looked a little hollow-eyed with the realization that they were losing one of the best among them–a strategist, a field marshal…

…a person you wanted beside you in a fight.

HOW CAN I HELP?

When it came time for dancing, they drained their glasses and took to the floor with abandon.

Speaker Pelosi cut a rug with an intern who'd brought along a guitar.

Don't I know it, kiddo.

You are one foxy speaker.

The kid composed an original song about Barney and sang it when everyone was just drunk enough to think it was good.

This land is your land, this land is my land, from Bayonne, New Jersey, to the Cape Cod islands.

Another congresswoman boogied ebulliently, long limbs swooping, like a friendly pelican diving for breakfast.

And the governor danced with Dottie, who, despite getting up in years, looked as graceful as she must've forty years earlier.

Governor, when Kerry goes to State, we want that Senate seat.

No doubt.

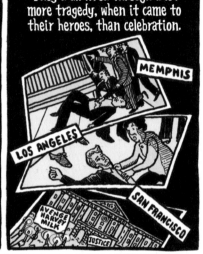

They'd all lived through a lot more tragedy, when it came to their heroes, than celebration.

MEMPHIS

LOS ANGELES

SAN FRANCISCO

AVENGE HARVEY MILK

JUSTICE

Hullo?

WHAT?

Yeah, I'll hold.

But here was Barney. He wasn't pretty. His personality wasn't always winning. He hadn't died young...

But he'd triumphed. He'd turned what could have been a life defined by sadness or fear or revulsion into one that was the opposite of those things.

And he'd accomplished important work, work that—when they squinted—helped them envision the kind of society that they hoped for.

Work that wasn't easy—and sure as hell wasn't glamorous—but that, if you thought about it, was heroic all the same.

And somehow he'd managed to offer them a perfect sense of timing—finishing the job at a new moment, when rather than *hiding*...

...or glossing over the fact of his love, they were all here, at his invitation, to help celebrate it.

And so they danced. Harder, and more joyously, all night long.

Eric Orner 2020

ACKNOWLEDGMENTS

Deepest thanks for their support and encouragement while I was writing and drawing this book to, among many others:

My mom, Rhoda Pierce

My brother, Peter Orner

My editor, Riva Hocherman, for taking a chance on this book

My agent, Rob McQuilken, for taking a chance on this career

Kelly Too at Metropolitan Books for production work on this book

Stephen T. Parks

Katie Crouch

Dave Zackin

Robert Dweck

Dave Vamos

Jennifer Camper

Civitella Ranieri

MacDowell

The Highland Park Illinois Public Library

Ardys Kozbial

Rob Kirby

Joan Hilty

Judy Dombrowski

Dr. David Brody

Jean Roslanowick

Bill Zavarello

Will Orner

Christopher J. Sullivan

Jane Kaplan

Tas Steiner

Armand LeBeau

James Maher

John Mahler

Ivan Averchenko

John Molner

Stella Johnson

Garth Patterson

Kevin Steen

Sharon DeLevie

Noam Nadav

Dan Gillis

Carlo Quispe

Thomas Henry Eagan

Catherine Pierce

Emilio Martí López

Harry Gural

Ted Abenheim

Justin Hall